Critical Thinking and Formative Assessments

Increasing the Rigor in Your Classroom

Betsy Moore
Todd Stanley

EYE ON EDUCATION
6 DEPOT WAY WEST, SUITE 106
LARCHMONT, NY 10538
(914) 833-0551
(914) 833-0761 fax
www.eyeoneducation.com

For information about permission to reproduce selections from this book, write: Eye On Education, Permissions Dept., Suite 106, 6 Depot Way West, Larchmont, NY 10538

Library of Congress Cataloging-in-Publication Data

Moore, Betsy.
   Critical thinking and formative assessments : increasing the rigor in your classroom / Betsy Moore and Todd Stanley.
      p. cm.
   ISBN 978-1-59667-126-3
1. Critical thinking--Study and teaching. I. Stanley, Todd. II. Title.
   LB1590.3.M66 2009
   370.15′2--dc22

                                                              2009022365

10 9 8 7 6 5 4 3

Also Available from Eye On Education

Short-Cycle Assessment:
Improving Student Achievement through Formative Assessment
Dr. Susan Lang, Todd Stanley and Betsy Moore

Rigor is NOT a Four-Letter Word
Barbara R. Blackburn

Teacher-Made Assessments:
Connecting Curriculum, Instruction, and Student Learning
Christopher R. Gareis and Leslie W. Grant

Differentiated Assessment for Middle and High School Classrooms
Deborah Blaz

Differentiating Assessment in Middle and High School
Mathematics and Science
Sheryn Spencer Waterman

Differentiating Assessment in Middle and High School English and Social Studies
Sheryn Spencer Waterman

Formative Assessment: Responding to Your Students
Harry Grover Tuttle

Formative Assessment for English Language Arts:
A Guide for Middle and High School Teachers
Amy Benjamin

Engaging Teens in Their Own Learning:
8 Keys to Student Success
Paul J. Vermette

Teaching, Learning, and Assessment Together:
The Reflective Classroom
Arthur Ellis

Handbook on Differentiated Instruction for Middle and High Schools
Sheryn Spencer Northey

Dedication

This book is dedicated to Dr. Jana Alig, who helped develop and implement many of the ideas and strategies found in this book and in the previous one.

Acknowledgements

We would like to thank all the teachers throughout Ohio with whom we have worked over the last several years to make lasting changes in instructional strategies with regard to critical thinking. We would especially like to thank the teachers from Nelsonville-York City Schools in Nelsonville, Ohio for training us in the trenches and having patience with us as we worked together to do what was best for students.

Thanks also to Deborah Fisher for her countless hours editing this book. In addition, we thank all of the people at Eye on Education for listening to our ideas and working with us to make our ideas come to fruition in this book.

Meet the Authors

Betsy Moore is a veteran teacher who retired from Reynoldsburg City Schools after 30 years of service and is currently the Executive Director of *Teacher 2 Teacher* (www.teacher2teacher.info), a national educational consulting company based in Ohio. Betsy began her career as a special education teacher, eventually moving on to the regular education classroom. While in the regular classroom she worked on many cutting-edge strategies including student-led conferences and short-cycle assessments. From 2000–2007 Betsy worked in the Literacy Curriculum Alignment Project (LCAP), training over 1500 teachers in more than 60 schools. She co-authored the book *Short-Cycle Assessment: Improving Student Achievement through Formative Assessment* which details the process developed in the LCAP work. In her role with *Teacher 2 Teacher*, Betsy provides quality professional development in the areas of differentiated instruction, short-cycle assessment development, and developing critical thinking skills and rigor to name a few. Betsy lives with her husband Dave, a retired high school assistant principal, in Columbus, Ohio. She has two grown children, Amy, who lives in Hilliard, Ohio, and Bryan, who lives in Temecula, California. Also living in Temecula is Betsy's first grandchild, a granddaugher, Aria Nicole.

Todd Stanley began teaching in 1997. A National Board Certified Teacher, he started out in the traditional classroom, teaching junior high students for two years, but quickly was given different growth experiences as a teacher. He taught on a gifted-accelerated team for three years, compacting three years of curriculum into two years of classroom time. He then taught at the Christopher Program, a project-based, integrated curriculum that serviced juniors and seniors, providing many outside learning experiences for students. During this time he also trained teachers from all around the state of Ohio for the Literacy Curriculum Alignment Project (LCAP), helping teachers to align their lessons to state standards and best prepare students for the state achievement tests. Next Todd created the Ivy Program, a pull-out gifted program for third and fourth graders, relying heavily on project-based learning. He currently teaches in the Reynoldsburg School District on the Quest Program, teaching Social Studies and Science to fifth and sixth graders and is the leader of the Critical Friends Group in his school. Todd lives in Pickerington, Ohio with his wife Nicki, and his two daughters, Anna and Abby.

Free Downloads

Beginning on page 77, you'll find a set of activities, blank forms, handouts and other documents called Blueprints to help you integrate critical thinking and rigor into your formative assessments. A selection of these documents is also available on Eye On Education's website in Adobe Acrobat ©. Those who have purchased this book have permission to print them out and duplicate them to distribute to your students.

You can access these downloads by visiting Eye On Education's website: www.eyeoneducation.com. Click on FREE DOWNLOADS or search or browse our website to find this book and then scroll down for downloading instructions. You'll need your book-buyer access code: CRI-7126-3.

List of Downloadable Blueprints

Table of Contents

Introduction:
Why Critical Thinking?

It is possible to store the mind with a million facts and still be entirely uneducated.

Alex Bourne

How do you teach thinking? The assumption is if you teach all the facts (the knowledge and the skills) thinking will simply occur as a natural extension of learning. This may happen occasionally with students who have a penchant for higher-level thinking, but with many students what you ask for is what you get. If you teach them facts, what you're going to get back are facts. If your focus is on basic skills, most likely that's what they'll show you.

This frame of learning is so ensconced in our educational system that even when you do ask for higher-level thinking, students may simply give you the lower-level knowledge they've accumulated over the years. If we want students to be able to think for themselves and access higher-level abilities, then as educators we have to be willing to take them there and show them how to do it.

Unfortunately like most things in education, this is easier said than done. We have hundreds of strategies for teaching rote memorization and knowledge-level learning. After all, this is probably the easiest method to teach, and it has produced results over many years of education. Now, however, the bar has been raised. We're no longer just competing on a local level with other students in our class—because of standardized testing we're competing with every student who attends school in the state and even in the country.

The call for increasing rigor in our classrooms is becoming more and more commonplace. With the world becoming smaller due to the advance of technology and the expansion of companies into a global market, we are also competing with people from all over the planet for spaces in colleges, for money, and for jobs. Today's students have to be able to do more than swallow facts and regurgitate them back out. They have to be quick on their feet, to adapt, and to roll with the punches. In short, they have to be able to think. This book approaches rigor from the standpoint of critical thinking and formative assessment, which is just one method. Many other ways to incorporate rigor into a classroom can be found in the book *Rigor Is Not a Four-Letter Word* by Barbara Blackburn, published by Eye On Education.

Corporations have caught on to the competitiveness of today's world and are demanding that students come to them with a different set of skills than were expected a generation ago. Rather than employees who can comprehend and apply, they're looking for people who can analyze and evaluate a situation. Because of this, states have adjusted their own standardized testing so the questions aren't simply asking for fact-based knowledge anymore. Many state tests are now including questions that require higher-level thinking skills. In essence, it is no longer enough to be able to tell *when* the Declaration of Independence was written or *who* wrote it; instead what's more important is *why* it was written and *how* it has affected history.

With this new theory of education in mind, this book was written *to show teachers how to teach students to think critically*. This isn't something that can be turned on and off like a switch. It's a process that takes time and patience. Students won't catch on to this type of thinking in the same way they do knowledge skills. Showing students that 2 + 2 = 4 is instant and gratifying for the students; requiring them to explain *how* 2 + 2 = 4 can be frustrating for students because they feel they've already given the correct answer. Critical thinking requires that you push students further than they are probably used to going, and this can initially cause discomfort for both them and you. It takes a special teacher to be willing to undertake this journey. Obviously, because you're reading this book, you are one of these special teachers.

The next thing this book will show you is *what higher-level thinking looks like*. For critical thinking to work, it must be engrained in the classroom. It's not something you can simply drop in any old place and expect it to work. It can be seen in the questions asked on formative assessments and class discussions. It should be used in the set up of assignments and the products that will demonstrate learning. We'll provide step-by-step directions that detail how to write higher-level questions, with the idea that once you learn this skill, you will be able to employ it throughout your curricula. We will also show how to write formative short-cycle assessments using higher-level thinking questions so that students will be prepared for the high-stakes testing that requires this same type of thinking.

Finally, getting students to think critically and access higher-level skills *will improve student achievement*. This will show itself on the high-stakes tests as well as in the classroom by the level your students will achieve in their day-to-day activities. Students will leave your classroom as stronger thinkers, better able to adapt to the higher-thinking world they'll encounter. You'll feel confident you've raised the level of rigor in your classroom, and you'll have the assessment data to prove it.

So how does a teacher learn to use critical thinking skills in the classroom? It must first start with an understanding of Bloom's Taxonomy, provided in Chapter 1 of this book. A brief review for those who are familiar with Bloom's is given, as well as a more detailed overview for those who are unfamiliar with it. Chapter 2 shows the clear differences between lower-level and higher-level thinking. It's important to be able to differentiate between these levels because many times teachers think they're teaching higher level skills when in fact they're simply using lower level thinking. Please note that lower level doesn't mean students aren't learning or being challenged; it simply indicates that the skills they're being asked to demonstrate don't require them to access critical thinking skills. Chapter 3 shows why critical thinking skills are so vital in education, especially with regard to state standardized testing and formative assessment. States are expecting more from students, and teachers must learn to adjust their classrooms to meet this expectation.

To best prepare students for high-stakes testing, it's important for you to be able to create your own assessments and questioning strategies. That leads us to Chapter 4, which demonstrates how to write lower-level thinking questions, those that assess knowledge, comprehension, and application. Then in Chapter 5 you will learn how to write higher-level thinking questions that look at the analysis, synthesis, and evaluation . All of this is then brought together in Chapter 6, where you learn to create and administer your own formative assessments to prepare students not only for high-stakes testing, but also for the skills necessary to be successful in life after school.

Because today's educator has to do more than just "teach to the test," Chapter 7 involves how to look at data from these formative assessments and figure out what adjustments need to be made in the classroom. It's important as educators to learn our students' strengths and weaknesses so we can respond where necessary. Chapter 8 provides concrete strategies for improving critical thinking in the classroom. For this to happen, you must be comfortable with higher level thinking skills, so be ready to learn right along with your students.

If you are diligent with students in this quest for higher-level thinking and push them to achieve, results *will* happen and students *will* learn at higher levels. We've seen this in our own classrooms and in many classrooms of teachers with whom we have worked. It's important to stay patient, and to know that in the long run, what you're doing is *what is best for students.*

1

Bloom's Taxonomy 101

The human mind is like a parachute—it functions better when it is open.

Cole's Rules

Bloom's Taxonomy

In today's educational world, the word "rigor" is rapidly coming to the forefront. Rigor is defined as "an environment in which each student is expected to learn at high levels, each student is supported so he or she can learn at high levels, and each student demonstrates learning at high levels" (Blackburn, 2008). As we try to prepare students for the twenty-first century it's become apparent we must do more than simply teach students facts; we must also teach them to think. Synonymous with the idea of rigor are the levels of thinking known as Bloom's Taxonomy. Most of us in the field of education have heard of Bloom's Taxonomy, whether we studied it in our undergraduate classes or maybe even dabbled in developing lessons and assessments attuned to a level of Bloom's. Like most things that are great in theory but hard to live out in day-to-day practice, the continued use of Bloom's Taxonomy, especially the higher levels of Bloom's, is challenging at best. There are a number of reasons for this.

First of all, in today's standards-based world, we as educators are faced with an overwhelming amount of content we must teach our students. Secondly, the emergence of high-stakes tests related to No Child Left Behind *(2001 Public Law 107-110)* has made us feel that our main undertaking needs to be preparing students for the yearly assessments. Finally, actually instilling in our students the ability to think at a higher level requires that we're able to understand, teach, and apply creative thinking skills ourselves. Because this is probably not the way most of us were taught,

1

our own critical thinking skills may be sorely lacking—and the bottom line is that it actually takes *using* higher-level critical thinking skills to *teach* higher-level critical thinking skills.

As we try to add rigor to our classroom practices, the logical question becomes "What is meant by higher-level critical thinking skills?" To really answer that question we need to review Bloom's Taxonomy in depth.

The History of Bloom's Taxonomy

Bloom's Taxonomy was developed in 1956 and followed the work of Benjamin Bloom and the three domains of learning:

> The cognitive—knowledge-based domain, consisting of six levels;
>
> The affective—attitudinal-based domain, consisting of five levels; and
>
> The psychomotor—skills-based domain, consisting of six levels.

Bloom's Taxonomy deals with the first domain—the cognitive domain. It was initially developed for use by university professors but was quickly adopted by curriculum planners, administrators, researchers, and classroom teachers from all levels of education (Anderson & Sosniak, 1994). It's become the leading model for critical thinking skills and because of this, we'll use Bloom's Taxonomy as we integrate higher-level thinking and rigor into formative, short-cycle assessments.

What Exactly is Bloom's Taxonomy?

Knowing that "taxonomy" is another word for "classification" is crucial to understanding Bloom's—it's simply a classification system of cognitive thinking skills. These skills are on a tier so that each one builds on the one before it; you cannot climb a flight of steps without first hitting the bottom ones, and so it goes with Bloom's. The better you understand the lower levels of thinking, the easier it will be to achieve the higher levels.

The six levels of Bloom's Taxonomy are:

```
                                                              Evaluation

                                                  Synthesis

                                        Analysis

                              Application

                  Comprehension

      Knowledge
```

Each of these levels is a descriptor for a particular way of thinking. An important thing to remember is a level of thinking at the lower end of the tier does *not* mean that type of thinking is any easier—it is simply different and less complex than some of the others. We'll go into more detail about how to distinguish lower-level thinking from higher-level thinking in the next chapter.

Knowledge

The knowledge level of Bloom's Taxonomy is considered to be the lowest level, and is probably the one with which we educators are most familiar. The descriptor of the knowledge level provided in most of the work associated with Bloom's is, "exhibits memory of previously learned material by recalling facts, terms, basic concepts, and answers" (based on Bloom's Taxonomy—developed by Linda G. Barton, M.S.Ed., 1997; hereafter cited as Bloom's Taxonomy/L. Barton, 1997). This is the type of learning demonstrated when educators ask their students to list things they have memorized or to answer basic, literal questions. Falling into this category are such things as memorizing all of the U.S. states for social studies or the multiplication tables for math. These are both knowledge-level skills. As an English teacher, you may ask your students to identify the main character in a novel—once again, knowledge level.

Bloom's often provides key words that represent this level. They include words such as *who, what, why, when, where, which, choose, find, how, define, label, show, spell, list, name, select, and tell.*

Comprehension

The second level of Bloom's Taxonomy is the comprehension level. The descriptor for this level is to "demonstrate understanding of facts and ideas by organizing, comparing, translating, interpreting, giving descriptions, and stating main ideas" (Bloom's Taxonomy/L. Barton, 1997). This is what we're doing when we ask our students to explain something—how they got an answer, or how they worked a problem. What this looks like is when we ask students to demonstrate what's just been taught to them, almost a restatement, just to be sure they understand it. When we were in school, this was the level we were working at when we wrote a book report and stated the main idea without any opinions. "Just the facts, ma'am" would be the motto of comprehension.

The words usually considered key at this level include *compare, contrast, demonstrate, interpret, explain, extend, illustrate, infer, outline, relate, rephrase, restate, translate, summarize, show, and classify.*

Application

Level three in Bloom's Taxonomy is the application level. According to Bloom, this level requires the learner to "solve problems to new situations by applying acquired knowledge, facts, techniques, and rules in a different way" (Bloom's Taxonomy/L. Barton, 1997). Application is what we're asking from students when we ask them to solve a math problem using a formula or a specific strategy when the problem is one they have not seen previously. It's different from memorization or restatement of facts because students have to take the fact and apply it to something new. It's also what a social studies student does when he reads a map and uses the scale. He has been taught how to use the scale, but has not been taught the specific distance between the two points; the student needs to apply the scale-reading skills to answer the problem. If you ever wrote a Haiku poem when you were in school and used the format involved (a non-rhyming poem where the first line contains five syllables, the second line seven syllables, and the third line five syllables), then you were working at an application level.

Some of the key words and phrases used when learning at the application level include *apply, build, choose, construct, develop, interview, make use of, organize, experiment with, plan, select, solve, identify,* and *model.*

Analysis

Analysis is described in Bloom's Taxonomy as thinking that asks a student to "examine and break information into parts by identifying motives or causes; make inferences and find evidence to support generalizations" (Bloom's Taxonomy/L. Barton, 1997). This is what we ask students to do when we have them look at the main characters in two different stories and compare how they relate to one another. In science class, it's what happens when we ask students to classify common plants according to their characteristics. What it might look like are the questions on ability tests when a student is asked to complete the phrase, "hot is to cold as black is to _____."

Some of the key words and phrases employed when using analysis are *analyze, categorize, classify, compare, contrast, discover, dissect, divide, examine, inspect, simplify, survey, take part in, test for, distinguish, distinction, relationships, function, motive, inference, assumption,* and *conclusion.*

Synthesis

The definition of synthesis in Bloom's is to "compile information together in a different way by combining elements in a new pattern or proposing alternative solutions" (Bloom's Taxonomy/L. Barton, 1997). We ask students to synthesize when we direct them to write a different ending to a story. Another example of synthesis is when we ask students to propose a new solution to a problem involving a current issue; for example, global warming. Synthesis may be the most challenging of the levels in Bloom's to understand, the reason being in core areas of school we don't focus as much on creativity as we do on comprehension. How often do students create something new in social studies class or in mathematics class? Usually they're simply hunting for a single correct answer. Synthesis allows students to create new knowledge and information as they take apart new material.

According to Bloom's, some of the key words to consider when using synthesizing are *build, choose, combine, compile, compose, construct, create, design, develop, estimate, formulate, imagine, invent, make up, originate, plan, predict, propose, solution, suppose, discuss, modify, change, original, improve, adapt, minimize, maximize, delete, theorize, elaborate, test, improve, happen, and change.*

Evaluation

The evaluation level of Bloom's is one that seems to be a little more comfortable for most of us because what we know about opinions is that everyone has one! Evaluation is defined as the type of learning demonstrated when a student is asked to "present and defend opinions by making judgments about information, validity of ideas or quality of work based on a set of criteria" (Bloom's Taxonomy/L. Barton, 1997). This can be as simple as a child telling the kindergarten teacher why blue is his favorite color. It's what children do when they choose which book is their favorite and tell why they chose it. Another example of evaluation is choosing a side on a current issue in social studies and defending that side. Teachers tend to use this higher level more frequently than analysis and synthesis simply because it's a level with which they are more familiar.

According to Bloom's, some of the key words central to the level of evaluation are *award, criticize, determine, judge, compare, recommend, agree, opinion, support, prove, estimate, choose, decide, dispute, justify, mark, rule on, appraise, interpret, importance, disprove, perceive, influence, conclude, defend, evaluate, measure, rate, select, prioritize, explain, criteria, assess, value, and deduct.*

The "New" Bloom's Taxonomy

Bloom's Taxonomy has held up very well since it was developed in 1956. There have been a number of variations of the taxonomy, and even a few revisions as well. The most notable revision was developed by Lorin Anderson, who was a former student of Benjamin Bloom and who led a team to update the taxonomy in the 1990s. The "new" Bloom's Taxonomy was published in 2001 and reflects a few minor changes. One of the main changes has to do with the terminology—instead of using nouns, the new Bloom's uses verbs. The reasoning behind this is that verbs describe actions, and Anderson believed that as educators in the twenty-first century continued to use Bloom's it was important to remember that thinking is an active process. As we traverse the age of information in the twenty-first century, our thinking cannot remain stagnant. "Stand still" learning is quickly making way for "continued learning," and the new Bloom's taxonomy with verbs makes the process a more active one.

Below is a list of the new levels of Bloom's Taxonomy:

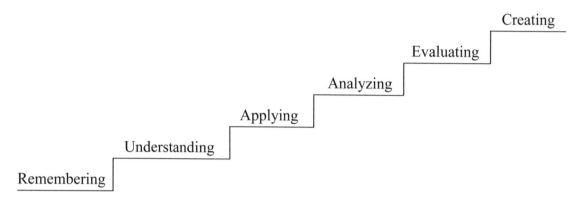

To better understand the similarities and differences of the "old" Bloom's Taxonomy and the new Bloom's, please reference the chart in the Blueprints section of this book entitled, *The Old Bloom's and the New Bloom's: What's the Diff???*

For the purposes of this book we will use the original Bloom's. If you're more familiar with the new, revised Bloom's, as you integrate critical thinking into formative assessments please feel free to use that version; the basic step-by-step process will remain the same no matter which you choose.

The "Critical" Part of Bloom's Taxonomy 101

The call for rigor is becoming more and more pronounced in the twenty-first century. This has brought the use of Bloom's Taxonomy back into the classroom. Bloom's is a tiered model of classifying levels of thinking. It contains six levels, beginning with what's considered to be the lowest level of thinking and progressing to more complex levels. The six levels of thinking and what they involve are:

1. *Knowledge*—recalling basic facts and concepts.
2. *Comprehension*—demonstrating understanding of something learned.
3. *Application*—using information already learned in a new way.
4. *Analysis*—breaking information into parts and examining those parts by looking for relationships.
5. *Synthesis*—taking something apart and creating something new.
6. *Evaluation*—judging something based on a set of criteria.

Analysis, synthesis, and evaluation are considered to be the higher levels of thinking and thus are invaluable tools for integrating critical thinking into both curriculum and formative assessments. The idea is to provide your students with the rigor necessary to be successful both today and in tomorrow's world.

2

Lower-Level Thinking and Higher-Level Thinking: What's the Difference?

Intelligence is something we are born with. Thinking is a skill that must be learned.

Edward de Bono

There Is a Difference

For educators in the 1980s, critical thinking was not something many stressed. There was a lot of memorization from the state capitals and periodic table to the multiplication tables and spelling words. As we approached the twenty-first century and the "Information Age," the ability to problem-solve became more and more important, especially as reports from large corporations continually criticized schools for failing to provide workers who had the ability to think critically. That and the introduction of standards-based education, high-stakes testing, and the call for rigor led many educators to begin a journey into the world of critical thinking.

It was disheartening to find that many students could not answer questions that involved higher-level thinking once asked to do so. It became very clear that the higher-level thinking puzzle needed to be solved sooner rather than later. That

7

realization led educators back to Bloom's Taxonomy and how to tell the difference between higher-level and lower-level thinking.

There seems to be a great deal of confusion over what constitutes higher-level thinking. This chapter is designed to eliminate some of the confusion.

Lower-Level Thinking

According to Bloom's, the first three levels—*knowledge, comprehension,* and *application*—are all lower, or entry-level thinking. Many educators mistakenly think that any time students have to come up with an answer in their heads, without it being directly in front of them, they are participating in higher-level thinking. This belief may lead teachers to go back and change multiple choice questions into fill-in-the-blank questions or to give essay questions instead of matching to achieve higher-level thinking. There are two problems with this. First of all, the type of thinking involved is definitely not higher level, and second, even if it were, students are rarely taught *how* to answer the questions. To change the way students think, educators need to change their own thinking.

In examining and studying the levels of thinking, it's easy to understand why knowledge is lower level. This is what happens when students are asked to identify something, recite something that has been memorized, list things, or even define something. An easy way to demonstrate the knowledge level of Bloom's Taxonomy is to study a question that requires this type of thinking. We'll do this by using the story of *The Three Little Pigs*. A knowledge-level question using this story would be:

Which house was the Big Bad Wolf unable to blow down?
>   A. The house made of sticks
>   B. The house made of bricks
>   C. The house made of mud
>   D. The house made of straw

This question requires students to exhibit memory of previously learned material. The answer is right in the text. There's no extraneous thinking going on.

The second level of Bloom's—comprehension—is also considered to be lower level. Many times this is a surprise because it's thought that if students are asked to explain why or how, they're using higher-level thinking skills. What they're actually being asked to do is demonstrate that they understand something.

You can probably correctly identify a microwave oven. You can also correctly use a microwave oven as well, knowing what buttons to push to operate it. But, can you explain how a microwave oven works? What causes it to cook the food? (The answer is not just microwaves, by the way.) What this demonstrates is that you learned the name of the microwave oven, but you don't understand how it works. Understanding how a microwave oven works doesn't lead to higher-level thinking, however. It just means you were told by someone or read it on the Internet—you learned it. As complex as that answer seems, it's still merely a lower-level comprehension response.

The following is a question from *The Three Little Pigs* asked at the comprehension level of Bloom's:

> **What did the Big Bad Wolf do when he could not blow down the third little pig's house? Explain why he did this.**

This question not only asks the reader to identify the action—going down the chimney—but it goes one step further and asks the reader to explain why the wolf did what he did. As you can see, the first part of the question is at a knowledge level, while the second part is at a comprehension level. Many times educators stop after the first part of the question and don't delve into the level of understanding. It's assumed that if students can answer the "what," they automatically know the "why." A first step toward leading students to higher-level thinking would be to simply go to the next step of the comprehension level with students on a regular basis and always ask why.

Even though the comprehension level of thinking requires more of students, it's still considered lower-level thinking. That's because it still deals with a concrete answer. That's not to say it's easy for the students—and that's something that must be stressed over and over. Lower level does not mean easy; it's simply a way of thinking that involves a different skill set than higher-level thinking does.

The third level of Bloom's Taxonomy—application—is the last level considered to be lower level. This almost always comes as a real surprise to many educators. It's often felt that if students are actually using what they learned, they have to be taking their thinking to a higher level. The reason this level is considered to be lower level is that, simply put, it is what it is. There's only one way to apply the steps of subtraction with borrowing. It can be done with different numbers, but the process remains the same. Some people argue that there are different ways to subtract with regrouping, and sometimes students can do it a different way and still come up with the correct answer, but that statement shows exactly why it is still lower level—there's only one correct answer. The process might change somewhat, but the basic premise as well as the answer remains the same.

Now, let's apply this to *The Three Little Pigs*. The following is an example of an application question:

> **Apply the lesson learned in *The Three Little Pigs* to an architect constructing a modern skyscraper. Specifically, whose house should the architect model his skyscraper after and why?**

The reason this is an application question is that students are being asked to apply what they already know and understand about the lesson to a modern-day situation.

It goes a step further than the comprehension level—being able to explain what the lesson is—and requires slightly deeper thinking (we like to call application "higher lower-level thinking"). The reason this is still considered lower level is that it takes an idea or concept that's already been learned and shows deepened understanding by putting it in a new situation. The basic concept still remains what it is, however. One final point to remember: You cannot apply what you've learned unless you know it and understand it. One level builds upon the next. Think of it as scaffolding.

Higher-Level Thinking

Higher-level thinking is also known as critical thinking or higher-order thinking. It involves using reasoning skills, both deductive and inductive. Other adjectives found when searching for a definition for critical thinking include *comparing, classifying, sequencing, patterning, web forecasting, hypothesizing, and critiquing,* just to name a few. In Bloom's Taxonomy, the three levels that require higher-level thinking are *analysis, synthesis,* and *evaluation.*

When trying to determine levels of thinking, analysis is the level that's perhaps the most misused. That's because many times the perception is it must be higher-level thinking when it involves something that's difficult or challenging for students. Consequently, the thinking is that because it's difficult, students have to analyze.

Analysis specifically requires students to break apart information—the analyze part—and examine how the parts relate to one another. It's like digging through a pile of dirt, looking at the different components, and determining how they work together to form a plant. It's more than merely studying something. The other important part of the analysis level is that students need to make inferences when things are not entirely literal or clear and then find evidence to support these generalizations. Analysis is what investigators on the *CSI* television shows are doing when they look at evidence at a crime scene and try to deduce how the crime took place from these clues.

Going back to *The Three Little Pigs,* an analysis question about that story would look like this:

> **Think about the lessons told in the following stories. Which story relates most closely to the lesson in *The Three Little Pigs* and why?**
>
> A. *Goldilocks and the Three Bears* because Goldilocks was not careful when she ate the porridge.
>
> B. *The Tortoise and the Hare* because the one who was the most careful and did the best job won.
>
> C. *Little Red Riding Hood* because the wolf tricked Red Riding Hood.
>
> D. *Jack and the Beanstalk* because Jack built a beanstalk like the pigs built their houses.

This question requires students to examine and study the lesson learned in the story *The Three Little Pigs* and then figure out the relationship between that lesson and the lessons in other stories. Students must decide which story's lesson is most like the lesson learned in *The Three Little Pigs* (by the way, the correct answer to the question is B, because the character that did the best and most careful job came out ahead). Throughout this process the students need to make inferences, and even more importantly, find evidence to support their generalizations. You can "feel" how this question is different from a question that asks students to choose the lesson learned; this question requires a lot of extraneous thinking, or in other words, complex thinking. Sometimes the criteria for categorizing levels of thinking into lower level or higher level is simply a matter of feel—higher-level questions really do feel different than lower-level questions.

The fifth level of Bloom's Taxonomy—synthesis—is a little easier to identify but difficult to instruct and evaluate. Synthesis requires students to put information together in a different way to get something new. This level is often confused with application, mostly because they're both thought of as making something new by putting things together. The difference is application takes something learned and uses it in the same way in a new situation, while synthesis is making up a whole new and different product by taking apart the information (analysis) and putting it back together as something completely new. This is what you'd do if you were going to take the components of several different types of roses and make a totally new and unique type of rose—one that had never been grown before. Synthesis is what we ask students to do when we ask them to rewrite the ending of a story or propose a new solution to an existing problem. In *The Three Little Pigs* scenario, a synthesis question would look like this:

> **What is one thing you could change in the plot of *The Three Little Pigs* so the story ends in a different way? Describe the change and explain in detail how this would alter the ending of the story.**

The reason this is a synthesis question is that students not only have to take what they know and understand about plot, but they must also apply the concept in a different way to make a new ending. In the process, they have to analyze what would make the ending different or how it could change.

This example may be a little easier to understand than the analysis example, but synthesis is many times harder to instruct. The assessment of synthesis is also difficult because there can be more than one correct answer.

The final level of Bloom's Taxonomy—evaluation—is perhaps the "easiest" level of the ones considered to be higher level. This is because it is the level of higher-order thinking with which we typically have a lot of experience. Evaluation requires students to make an opinion about something based on a set of criteria. The latter part of the definition, "based on a set of criteria," is what makes this level challenging. The opinion needs to fit the criteria, but it can still be (and needs to be) an original thought. The students aren't tied down to one correct answer, which can be difficult for teachers to assess. What must be looked at is the criteria and the evidence provided.

An example of an evaluation question using *The Three Little Pigs* would be:

> **Do you think the story of *The Three Little Pigs* should be changed to relate better to the twenty-first century? Explain why or why not. Be sure to defend your opinion by stating how the story does or does not currently relate to the twenty-first century.**

Here, students are being asked to give their opinion about the story, with the criterion being how it relates to the twenty-first century. Again, whether or not this question is correct will depend on the justification of the answer. This is not just about expressing an opinion. Students need to know and understand the plot of the story, be able to use the concept of plot, be able to analyze the parts of the plot, be able to put it together in a new way, and then be able to evaluate the two versions. You can see how one level builds on the previous one.

The last point to be made with regard to lower-level and higher-level thinking is higher-level thinking is *not* developmental. We can use higher-level thinking at a very early age. Toddlers use higher level thinking skills as they acquire language—they're constantly having to analyze, synthesize, and evaluate. These examples using *The Three Little Pigs* seem to be tailored to older students. We've provided examples of higher-level questions using different fairy tales that can be used with younger students in *Higher-Level Questions for Younger Learners* in the Blueprints section of this book.

The Final Way of Thinking

The more work you do with Bloom's Taxonomy and the different levels of thinking, the better you will become at distinguishing the levels, and in fact developing questions and lessons around these levels of thinking. This will take a lot of practice but will serve to raise the rigor in the classroom. Prior to that, you might want to consider starting off by simply labeling your questions as lower or higher level. Many times you can determine which type of a question you are asking without actually breaking the question down and classifying it as a specific level of Bloom's—although that's definitely the best way to learn the levels.

In the beginning, we'd suggest looking at the questions in your daily lesson plans, or on your classroom assessments and/or quizzes, and try to sort them into the categories of lower-level thinking or higher-level thinking. We've provided a tool for you entitled *What Level of Thinking Is It?* in the Blueprints section of this book. If you are having trouble with the six specific levels of Bloom's, this would be a good way to begin changing your way of thinking.

The "Critical" Part of Lower-Level Thinking and Higher-Level Thinking

Critical thinking involves a more complex way of thinking. Sometimes you can feel the difference between lower- and higher-level thinking questions. According to Bloom's Taxonomy, the first three levels—*knowledge, comprehension,* and *application*—involve lower-level thinking. This is not to say this type of thinking is easy, it just involves a more literal way of thinking. The last three levels of Bloom's Taxonomy—*analysis, synthesis,* and *evaluation*—all involve higher-level thinking. These require students to use reasoning skills and to "think outside the box," moving away from literal answers. The correct answer isn't as apparent in these types of questions. That doesn't mean they're harder than lower-level questions, but rather that they involve a different type of thinking skill.

It's sometimes easier to begin integrating higher-level thinking into your lessons and assessments by examining what you currently do and categorizing that into two categories—lower level or higher level. As you continue to work with the different levels of Bloom's and you increase your practice in higher-level activities, you'll be able to define those activities into a specific level of Bloom's.

Higher-level thinking is not developmental—students at all ages can do it. Like anything else, it is a matter of practice. We can't expect students to be good at something they have little or no experience with; after all, that would be like expecting someone to swim before he or she has been taught how. The rate of success would be very low. To become proficient in thinking at a critical or higher level, students have to be exposed to and provided practice in this type of thinking. It's only through the intentional teaching of critical thinking that we'll raise the level of rigor for all students.

3

How Do Critical Thinking Skills Enhance Student Achievement?

You are today where your thoughts have brought you. You will be tomorrow where your thoughts take you.

James Allen

Why Critical Thinking?

In the world of No Child Left Behind and high-stakes testing, questions that ask *why* and *how* naturally come to mind.

- Why teach higher-level critical thinking skills to students when schools are judged by paper and pencil assessments?

- How exactly will raising the rigor in our classrooms benefit our students in their school lives, as well as beyond school?

- Isn't the ability to think at a higher level limited to those students with higher cognitive abilities?

- How can we ask younger students to think at higher levels when they don't seem to be developmentally ready?

14

The answers to these questions make up the essential elements of the rationale for teaching higher-level critical thinking skills to students of all ages and ability levels. Let's examine them one at a time.

Developmental Readiness

One of the arguments heard most often with regard to teaching higher-level critical thinking skills to young children is that it's not "developmentally appropriate." This is mostly due to the fact some educators believe the brain must be fairly developed through years of schooling to think at a higher level. When this assumption is examined more closely, however, it becomes evident that there are gaping holes in it.

Let's look a little more closely at the example provided in the previous chapter—the acquisition of language. An 18-month old child is learning to talk. As the ability to communicate strengthens, the child needs to employ all kinds of higher-level thinking. First he has to learn a word—"no," for example (a common one most parents can relate to). To learn the word, the child first needs to think at a *knowledge* level. He may hear an older sibling use the word, and then simply mimic it back— basic recall. Next, the child needs to understand the word. To do this, he needs to think at a *comprehension* level. He interprets the word "no" to mean he doesn't want something. Then the child needs to have practice applying the word. He may have heard a sibling tell his parent "no" when a request was made to turn off the television. The child now applies that response to a different situation: When the parent asks him to put away a toy and come to dinner, he responds with the word "no." He's demonstrating that he can use the word in a new and different context at the *application* level.

Next, the child will analyze his use of the word "no" by examining the relationship between that word and the response it gets. For example, he may see that when he responds with "no" he's promptly put in time-out—a negative response. Or the word "no" may result in his being able to play for a while longer—a positive response. Or, the child may receive one response from one parent, and the complete opposite from the other parent. Whichever way this goes may impact how the child chooses to use the word in the future. The point is that the child begins to analyze the situation, trying to find generalizations and relationships, which is the basis for the *analysis* level of critical thinking. If the child doesn't like the response he got when he said "no" to putting away the toy, maybe he'll try a different approach, such as changing "no" to "no, thank you." In this way he's thinking at a *synthesis* level—combining elements together in a new way. This will lead him to the final level of critical thinking—*evaluation*. At this point, the child will judge which of the two responses worked better for him. If he determines that "no, thank you" works better than "no," it's because he truly understands that "no, thank you" got him what he wanted better than "no" did. Of course a toddler can't express this verbally at 18 months old, but it isn't because he's not at that level of thinking.

Cognitive Ability and Critical Thinking

In the same way some people believe young children cannot think at a critical or higher level, many also believe the only groups that can think at these levels are the cognitively gifted. When pondering critical thinking and students who are limited cognitively, it helps to think of a sports analogy. There are undoubtedly people born with the natural ability to play basketball very well, given the inborn skills of coordination, jumping ability, and speed; and then there are those without the proverbial "athletic bone" in their bodies. That doesn't mean the person without natural skill can't learn how to make a free throw. Even the most unskilled person is going to get better at free throws if he's shown how to shoot the free throw, is exposed to this technique over and over, and practices constantly—even if he never quite reaches the level of the person who's naturally gifted at such a skill.

This is not to say the cognitively disabled student can think at the same critical thinking level as the gifted student. Just as there are different levels of physical development, there are different levels of critical thinking, some more complex than others. What's been shown time and time again is that raising the rigor, no matter what the circumstance, almost always results in increased achievement. How many times have you read about the parents of a cognitively delayed child requiring more of that child than anyone thought was possible? The ultimate result is usually that the child has performed above expectations. If this is the case with disabled children, can you imagine what might happen if we raised the rigor for all students? Simply put, teaching all students to think at a higher level, and then giving these students practice in thinking at a higher level, benefits everyone. Students will become better thinkers not just for the duration of their school experience, but also in their lives beyond the classroom.

Critical Thinking Skills and Higher Achievement

Research shows there's a link between critical thinking skills and increased student achievement in the classroom. In one study conducted by the National Assessment of Educational Progress (NAEP), assessments were given to a cross-range of students. These assessments were derived from representative samples of students in the 4th, 8th, and 12th grades throughout the United States (U.S. Department of Education, 2001). In his study of these test scores, Harold Wenglinsky found that teaching critical thinking is associated with higher test scores (Wenglinsky, 2000, 2002, 2003). Wenglinsky went on to state that, "Instruction emphasizing advanced reasoning skills promotes high student performance" (Wenglinsky, 2004).

Many believe critical thinking skills should be limited to those subject areas that lend themselves to it, such as English, but these learning skills *can* be taught across the curriculum. For example, studies show that if critical thinking and higher reasoning skills were taught in the areas of mathematics and science, then the achievement levels in these subjects would go up. This statement is supported by a study that TIMSS (The Trends in International Mathematics and Science Study) performed in which videotapes of 8th grade classrooms in the United States, Germany, and Japan were analyzed. The study found that Japanese 8th grade teachers were more likely to emphasize critical thinking skills at an early age, and that overall, Japanese students outperformed their U.S. and German counterparts in mathematics (Stigler and Hiebert, 1999). This research supports the NAEP results, which suggest that although basic skills are important, critical thinking skills are essential. In mathematics and science at both the 4th and 8th grade levels, practices that emphasize critical thinking skills are associated with higher student achievement, whereas practices that emphasize basic skills are not (Wenglinsky, 2004).

Critical Thinking and High-Stakes Tests

Of course, in this time of No Child Left Behind, one of the overriding criteria for anything taught in our classrooms has to be the effect it will have on our students' meeting the standards mandated by their state. Looking at whether or not critical thinking skills were being assessed in the state tests yields mixed results. It seems that in some states, the required assessments contain many questions asking students to think at a higher level, whereas in other states, the assessments are mostly assessing lower-level knowledge material. For example, the following is a question found on the 5th grade mathematics assessment from Texas (TAKS: Texas Assessment of Knowledge and Skills):

Tuna Fish Cans

Number of Cans	Total Height (millimeters)
2	76
5	190
8	304
10	380

The table above shows the total height in millimeters of different stacks of tuna fish cans. What is the relationship between the number of cans and the total height in millimeters?

A. The total height in millimeters is 76 more than the number of cans.

B. The total height in millimeters is 76 times the number of cans.

C. The total height in millimeters is 38 times the number of cans.

D. The total height in millimeters is 38 more than the number of cans.

This question is assessing students at the analysis level of thinking. If students who take this test are not taught how to answer critical thinking questions, then they'll be hard pressed to be successful on a question such as this.

At the other end of the spectrum are those tests with questions asked at a very low level of thinking. For example, consider this science question from the Oregon Assessment of Knowledge and Skills (OAKS):

A frog is a vertebrate that can also be classified as:

A. an amphibian.

B. a fish.

C. a reptile.

D. an arthropod.

This particular question is asked at a very low level of recall. A student either knows it or doesn't. No amount of critical thinking is going to help with a question such as this. A student will need to have a teacher instruct him in this or he'll have to read it in a book somewhere. Even the title of the test, OAKS, focuses on Knowledge and Skills, very much in the lower area of Bloom's.

Some states use a mixture of higher and lower-level questions on their tests. An example of this can be found on the Ohio 8th Grade Social Studies Achievement Test.

Which belief do Jews and Muslims share?

A. Mecca is a holy city.

B. There is only one God.

C. Jesus is the son of God.

D. There are many paths to truth.

Although this is a challenging question, it is lower-level recall. It might suggest that students need not know how to think at a higher level. That would be a false assumption, however, if one were to look at some of the other questions on this assessment. The following question is found on the same assessment and reflects a very different type of thinking:

> The... speedy removal [of the Indians]... will place a dense and civilized population in large tracts of country now occupied by a few savage hunters.... What good man would prefer a country covered with forests and ranged by a few thousand savages to our extensive Republic, studded with cities, towns and prosperous farms... occupied by more than 12,000,000 happy people, and filled with all the blessings of liberty, civilization and religion?
>
> —President Andrew Jackson, 1830

Which of these statements reflects Andrew Jackson's attitude about American Indians and their lands?

A. He believed that American Indians could not take care of themselves.

B. He thought that American Indians might adapt to life on farms and in cities.

C. He believed that white settlers could make better use of the land than American Indians.

D. He thought that American Indians would be happier when they were removed to new lands.

This question from the Ohio Achievement Test obviously requires the student to perform higher-level thinking. It's not a simple comprehension question because nowhere in the text is Jackson's attitude stated. Instead this must be inferred using clues not directly in the text, making it an analysis question.

The point to be made here is although assessment of basic knowledge is still taking place, more and more state tests are moving toward the assessment of critical thinking skills. Therefore, raising the rigor in our classrooms makes a lot of sense. Critical thinking skills are not skills that can be studied or memorized. They are skills that must be learned — and for students to be successful on such assessments, these skills must be learned in the classroom. It is like the old Confucian saying, "Give a man a fish and you have fed him for a day. Teach a man to fish and you have fed him for a lifetime." What this means in terms of critical thinking skills is this: When teaching students a specific piece of knowledge, such as the different parts of an atom, they can answer only questions concerning that very topic. Teaching students how to think critically will enable them to answer nearly any critical thinking question they encounter, regardless of the topic.

Another equally important consideration when deciding whether or not to teach critical thinking skills is the issue of preparing students for the national assessments they are required to take to get into college. For example, consider this question taken from the SAT (formerly Scholastic Aptitude Test and Scholastic Assessment Test):

> **Which of the following best describes the difference between Passages 1 and 2?**
>
> A. Passage 1 remembers an event with fondness, while Passage 2 recalls a similar event with bitter detachment.
>
> B. Passage 1 considers why the author responded to the visit as he did, while Passage 2 supplies the author's reactions without further analysis.
>
> C. Passage 1 relates a story from a number of different perspectives, while Passage 2 maintains a single point of view.
>
> D. Passage 1 treats the visit to the theater as a disturbing episode in the author's life, while Passage 2 describes the author's visit as joyful.
>
> E. Passage 1 recounts a childhood experience, while Passage 2 examines how a similar experience changed over time.

To answer this question a student needs to be able to analyze, synthesize, and evaluate. The reader has to compare and contrast the two passages and then draw a conclusion based not on knowledge given directly in the text, but on a deduction within the content, sort of reading between the lines. It's also important to note that the SAT now includes a writing section, as well as sentence completion questions that truly limit students' ability to guess. Proficiency in critical thinking skills would be very beneficial for students taking an assessment of this nature.

Critical Thinking Skills and Life Beyond School

The argument may be made if you live in a state where the questions on the year-end assessment are mostly lower level, and most of your students do not go on to college, that there's no need to spend time on critical thinking skills in the classroom. Sometimes the instruction geared toward higher-level critical thinking skills is thought of only in terms of the college-bound student, but what about the student who isn't going to attend a four-year college? What about the student who will enter an apprenticeship or a trade school following graduation? What about the student who simply is going to go out right after high school and get a job?

A lot of information has been published lately from employers who state that incoming employees today don't seem to have the ability to think and solve problems. For example, according to a report titled, "Are They Really Ready To Work? Employers' Perspectives on the Basic Knowledge and Applied Skills of New Entrants to the 21st Century U.S. Workforce," prepared by a consortium of the Conference Board, Partnership for 21st Century Skills, Corporate Voices for Working Families, and the Society for Human Resource Management (April and May 2006), more than half of the employers (58%) stated that critical thinking and problem solving skills are "very important" for incoming high school graduates' successful job performance. Of these same employers, nearly three-quarters (70%) rated recently hired high school graduates as deficient in critical thinking.

The number of low-skilled, blue-collar jobs is shrinking as technology replaces workers who were once trained to do such tasks. We're going primarily from a product industry to a service industry, where critical thinking skills are a prerequisite for success. Regardless of educational background or placement upon graduation from high school, no one would argue that critical thinking skills *hinder* the ability of one's success in the work force. In fact, when faced with the day-to-day decision-making required of most jobs, one would argue that proficiency in critical thinking skills would actually *enhance* the ability of one's success in the work force, again reinforcing the idea that raising the rigor in schools makes sense.

The obvious implication here is that if schools are choosing *not* to focus on critical thinking skills, and choose instead to marshal their efforts toward lower-level, knowledge-based learning, they're doing their students a disservice in getting them ready for life after high school. How many times will you have to use an isosceles triangle or apply the atomic weight of cobalt once you receive your high school degree? Post high school, how often will you have to conjugate a verb or recall what treaty ended World War I? Such skills are not nearly as valuable as teaching students how to think and use those skills to problem-solve—not just those students who are going on to college, but rather any students who will enter today's work force.

The "Critical" Part of Critical Thinking Skills and Student Achievement

Learning how to think at a higher level isn't limited by the age or cognitive level of the child. As soon as they're born, babies have to use critical thinking skills as they learn all about the world. This is evidenced in a toddler's acquisition of language and his subsequent development. In addition, critical thinking skills can be taught to students with impaired cognitive abilities through modeling and practice, and raising the rigor for these students has been found to have a positive impact on their achievement.

The argument for teaching students critical thinking skills is further strengthened when we examine the link between these skills and increased student achievement as measured by both nationally standardized tests and state high-stakes tests. Studies show that teaching students how to think at a higher level results in higher test scores. This is becoming especially relevant as more of the state and national tests move toward questions that assess critical thinking skills.

And what about life after the school experience? Employers today are clamoring for the worker who can think through problems and solve them. This means that teaching students to think at a higher level could very well result in better career opportunities for them.

One further point to be made has to do with the idea some educators have with regard to rigor—they feel that making the curriculum "challenging" for the student equates to making it "hard." This gives rigor a negative connotation. In reality, we actually hold those we care about the most to the highest standards. Think of your own children and the number of times you have made them re-do their homework assignment because it did not meet *your* high standards, not their teacher's. Were you being "mean," or were you in fact paying your children the highest possible compliment: You believed in their ability to achieve at a high level and would support them in achieving that same level?

Given the amount of research that supports the teaching of critical thinking skills to students of all ages and abilities, the question should be altered from, "Why teach critical thinking skills?" to "Why not?"

4

How To Write Lower-Level Questions: Knowledge, Comprehension, and Application

Critical thinking is a lot harder than people think, because it requires knowledge.

Joanne Jacobs

What is Lower-Level Thinking?

Lower-level thinking involves the first three levels of Bloom's Taxonomy: *knowledge, comprehension,* and *application*. The reason these are considered lower level is because the type of thinking revolves around something that's already been learned; that is, no new or different thinking is taking place. That's not to say the "lower" in lower level implies the thinking is easy. If you have to memorize the Gettysburg Address, for instance, that's not an easy task. For some, learning the multiplication tables is a daunting endeavor as well. Try holding your own at the game show *Jeopardy* to see how challenging lower-level thinking can be at times.

You can also think of knowledge, comprehension, and application as "entry levels," because to think at a higher level you first need to master the lower three levels. For example, to analyze the effects World War II had on our economy today you have to *know* about World War II as well as *comprehend* it. Then, you need to *apply* that knowledge to economics and life today. Only after these things have been accomplished will you be able to *analyze* the relationship between World War II and the economy today. That's what makes these levels just as important as the higher levels; they are stepping stones to deeper learning. If you want to add rigor to your curriculum, you need to make sure your students understand the first three levels of thinking. That means *you* need to know how to ask and assess these types of questions. This chapter is going to address how to do this.

Knowledge Level

Knowledge is considered to be the "lowest" of the levels of Bloom's taxonomy. Knowledge questions are what you ask when you simply want to find out if students know or can recall something that's been taught previously. When asking knowledge-level questions you aren't determining whether students understand what it is they know; for instance, you can ask students if they can identify what a heart is, but it's an entirely different thing to ask them if they understand how it works. It's the difference between what, where, when, and who questions and how and why questions, which are the questions that often lead to enduring understanding. This is one of the dangers of asking only knowledge-level questions—the students may remember them just long enough to show you they know the answer, and then forget them completely.

The key words used when asking knowledge-level questions are:

> who   what   when   where   which   choose   find   how   define
> identify   label   show   list   name   tell   recall   select   spell   match

Using these words it's fairly easy to formulate knowledge-level questions: *Who discovered electricity? What is electricity? Where do we use electricity?*

Another prompt to use when creating a knowledge-level question is a question stem. For a knowledge-level question, that may include one of the following:

> Who is ...?   What is ...?   When did ...?   Which one did ...?   Where would ...?
> Choose the one that ...?   Find the one that ...?   How did ...?   Define... .
> Identify which one... .   Label the one(s) that... .   Can you list the three ...?
> Can you name the ones that ...?   Tell which... .   Can you recall ...?
> Can you select ...?   Can you spell ...?   Match the ones that... .

Knowledge-level questions can be asked in many types of formats. A common one is multiple choice. The following question is an example of a multiple choice knowledge-level question:

The United States is in which of the following continents?

A. Asia

B. North America

C. South America

D. Europe

Of course the answer is North America, but people are not born with this knowledge. Somewhere along the way someone pointed this out to them or they read it in a book, but it's now common knowledge, and they can recall it to answer the question.

Many times knowledge-based questions are those that teachers ask quickly to determine core knowledge. Some examples of core knowledge content are:

- memorizing formulas in math
- learning the sight words in reading
- learning the rules of grammar in writing
- reciting the scientific method
- knowing the continents and oceans on a map

When asking a knowledge-level question, the answers will range from one word to several sentences. The length is determined more by the amount of content you have asked for than by the construction of the response. For instance, if you ask for the names of all of the countries involved in World War I, you should expect over 100 answers. If you ask how many sides a triangle has you should expect a single answer. In other words you get what you ask for.

In addition, knowledge-level questions can be asked in a graphic organizer; in this case students would be expected to fill in a chart:

Fill in the missing months on this chart

January	
	August
March	September
April	
June	December

Knowledge-level answers won't provide the teacher with any indication of whether students understand a concept, and asking only knowledge questions won't elevate the rigor in your classroom. It's simply a matter of the students being able to remember and recite back something that's been taught.

If you are looking for an explanation of learning or evidence of learning, then knowledge-level questions won't be the appropriate type of questions to ask. Regardless, they're necessary for building the levels of thinking.

Comprehension Level

The next level of Bloom's, comprehension, is the level at which students are asked to show they understand what it is that has been taught. This is the level most teachers strive for after first introducing a skill or concept. Just like the knowledge level, comprehension is essential before students can move to the higher levels of thinking. If the students cannot understand something, it would be very difficult to apply, analyze, synthesize, or evaluate it. For that reason, comprehension is a very important level in the thinking process.

Unfortunately, comprehension is the level at which many educators stop when trying to raise the rigor in the classroom. They feel by asking students to explain what they know, they're providing challenging content. It certainly is more rigorous than knowledge-level thinking, but there are many higher levels of thinking to strive for while improving rigor in the classroom.

The key words used when asking comprehension level questions are:

compare   contrast   demonstrate   interpret   explain   extend   illustrate infer   outline   relate   rephrase   translate   summarize   show   classify

Integrating these words into questions is one easy way to develop a comprehension-level question: *Explain your answer. Compare the two characters. Demonstrate how day and night occur.*

Another easy way to generate a comprehension-level question is to use the following question stems:

How would you explain? How would you compare? How would you contrast? Restate in your own words… What is the main idea of…? What is meant by…? Which statements support…? Which is the best answer…? Explain your answer…? Show how you know… Can you illustrate how…? How would you rephrase…? How would you classify the type of…? What can you say about…? Describe…

Comprehension questions can appear in many different formats, from multiple choice to constructed response (see the activity titled *How To Write Multiple Choice*

Questions for All Levels of Thinking in the Blueprints section of this book for a template showing how to write these questions). The important thing to remember when writing or asking a comprehension question is that the answer provides evidence of understanding.

A constructed response question, or one in which students have to provide written answers, is perhaps the easiest way to assess understanding. Look at the constructed response question below.

Which of the following numbers are odd numbers? Explain your answer.

1, 2, 3, 4, 5, 6, 7, 8

Notice that the first part of the question is at the knowledge level, simply identifying the odd numbers. It's the second part of the question, where students must explain their answer, that demonstrates comprehension.

Now, consider this question about the setting of a story:

Describe the setting in the story.

By *describing* the setting instead of simply *identifying* the setting, students are demonstrating that they understand the concept of setting.

Comprehension-level questions can also be written using the multiple choice format.

Which of the following numbers is a prime number and why?

    A. 9 because it only has two factors, itself and 9

    B. 3 because it only has two factors, itself and 3

    C. 9 because it only has three factors, itself, 9, and 3

    D. 3 because it only has two factors, itself and 1

The reason this question is at a comprehension level is that by choosing the correct answer, students are demonstrating understanding of the term "prime number." Guessing the correct number by itself only narrows down the choices; to make the correct choice you have to understand how one arrives at that correct answer.

The answer to a comprehension question should show that students have an understanding of the topic, usually involving more than a few words. To really demonstrate enduring understanding, students should be able to show that understanding in multiple ways.

Simple strategies to use when writing or asking comprehension questions are:

• Ask students to explain how they got their answers.

• Have students restate the meaning of something in their own words.

- Have students show how they got their answers.
- Have students give another example of the same concept.

Comprehension is a very important level of thinking. Only when we truly understand something can we move on and apply that knowledge in other contexts.

Application Level

The third level of Bloom's Taxonomy is the application level. Many teachers strive to get students to this level, thinking it to be the top. Often this is where teachers feel that "the rubber meets the road," and thus they are satisfied once the students reach this point.

While the application level certainly involves more complex thinking than the knowledge level, it's still considered lower-level thinking because we are asking students to apply knowledge that has already been learned. In other words, the thinking is based on previously learned skills or concepts. The reason this level is higher than knowledge or comprehension is that students are asked to use the acquired knowledge and apply it to a new situation. As with the other two levels, this one is often associated with some key words, which are:

| use apply build choose construct develop interview make use of |
| plan utilize organize select model solve experiment with show |

Examples: *Use a pronoun in a sentence. Apply the concept of foreshadowing to the following. Choose which one best represents a climax to the story.*

It's important to realize that simply using these words will not create an application-level question. A question like this…

Choose who the main character is.

A. Huck

B. Tom

C. Becky

D. Injun Joe

…is still a knowledge-level question if the teacher at one point in class identified Huck as the main character. The questions have to be designed so that students are taking prior knowledge and applying it to something new—in other words, something they haven't previously been told. For example, if the teacher had taught students how to identify a main character using *The Scarlet Letter* and then asked them to apply what they learned to *The Adventures of Huckleberry Finn,* that would make it an application-level question.

In addition, there are a number of question stems that may be helpful when developing application questions. Some of those include:

How would you use...?   What examples can you find to...?

How would you solve _____ using what you have learned?

How would you show your understanding of...? Use facts or concepts to show... .

How would you apply what you learned to...? What approach would you use to...?

Give other examples of... . Use what you know to solve... . Solve the following... .

The types of answers generated by application questions demonstrate that students can solve problems in new situations using knowledge that has already been learned. It isn't doing something new with the knowledge—the knowledge or skill remains the same. Application questions are those in math in which students are asked to solve problems using a learned formula. For example, the following question...

Solve the problem.

$$\begin{array}{r} 5\,6\,7 \\ -\,2\,1\,8 \\ \hline \end{array}$$

... asks students to demonstrate that the formula for subtracting with regrouping can be applied to a new problem. In much the same way, the following question...

In the selection, the author uses the abbreviation "Ms." for "Miss." Give an example of another abbreviation and use it correctly in a sentence.

...asks students to demonstrate an understanding of abbreviations (comprehension) and then apply that concept by not only identifying another abbreviation (knowledge), but also using that abbreviation in a sentence (application).

As with the knowledge and comprehension levels, questions addressing the application level of thinking can be asked in different formats. The example below shows how a question requiring students to demonstrate application skills can be asked in a multiple choice format.

Applying the concept of *laissez-faire*, in which of the following economic systems would you find it?

   A. socialism

   B. communism

   C. capitalism

   D. industrialism

Notice that the definition of *laissez-faire* remains the same, but the situation is different. Students have to apply the knowledge of *laissez-faire* to answer a question about a new situation.

Response grid questions are questions that are frequently used on tests to require students to demonstrate application skills. For example, the following problem...

Solve 456 × 16.

...is an example of a response grid question in which students need to apply the strategy of multiplication to solve the problem. Rather than search for a possible correct answer out of four choices, students must apply their knowledge of the math formula and create the answer themselves.

Assessing the application level of thinking is often where educators stop. It's believed if students can apply what they know and understand, then enduring understanding has taken place. Just because students can apply something doesn't mean they can creatively problem-solve, however. Going above the application level of learning is a sure way to add rigor to your classroom. Application serves as a building block for these higher levels of thinking.

The "Critical" Part of Writing Lower-Level Questions

The three lower levels of thinking—*knowledge, comprehension,* and *application*—can be assessed using questions in many different formats. Teachers should develop questions in such a way as to assess the particular type of thinking they are seeking to measure. For example, a knowledge-level question should assess whether or not students can recall information that has been taught. The answers to these questions will be straightforward, with only the correct answer provided without explanation. The level of thinking known as comprehension is where students demonstrate understanding of what's been taught. This type of thinking includes explanations, descriptions, and summaries. Application is the type of thinking in which students demonstrate the ability to use knowledge that's been learned previously and apply that knowledge to new situations, keeping the basic knowledge the same.

Mastery of each of the first three levels of thinking is necessary to move to the next level. To apply information, one needs to know and comprehend the information. Likewise, each of the first three levels of thinking is a foundation for the critical, higher levels of thinking: *analysis, synthesis,* and *evaluation.* If you think of the process of adding rigor to your classroom as moving up the steps of a ladder, these first three levels of thinking—*knowledge, comprehension,* and *application*—are essential for moving up. Skipping steps can cause one to stumble.

5

How To Write Higher-Level Thinking Questions: Analysis, Synthesis, and Evaluation

Education's purpose is to replace an empty mind with an open one.
Malcolm S. Forbes

What is Higher-Level Thinking?

Higher-level thinking involves the latter three levels of Bloom's Taxonomy—*analysis, synthesis,* and *evaluation.* These are the levels of thinking synonymous with adding rigor to a curriculum. They're considered higher level because they involve extraneous thinking, or doing something other than just working with knowledge as it was taught—in other words, moving beyond basic knowing, understanding, and applying. Most people consider this type of thinking more difficult, but it also allows the learner to work without the usual constraints of conventional recall, and for some this makes it more motivating than pure memorization. Regardless, in a classroom where the teacher wishes to add rigor, one way to do it is to ask more higher-level

32

thinking questions, not just on assessments, but in the day-to-day practices of the classroom including discussion, homework, and other activities.

These levels are dependent on the acquisition of the three lower levels of thinking in Bloom's Taxonomy. They're also dependent upon one another as the thinker moves up the taxonomy hierarchy. For example, to analyze how the setting influences the plot of a story, you have to *know* and *comprehend* the basic concept of setting, then *apply* this information to plot. Using higher levels of thinking, you can then *analyze* what influence setting has had on the plot of a particular piece of writing by looking at the relationship between the setting and what happens in the story. Using *synthesis* skills, you can change the setting of the same story and determine how the change would influence the plot of the story. Finally, you can *evaluate* whether you think the change of setting would make the plot better or worse and why. As you can see, you cannot move to the higher levels of thinking without first mastering the lower ones. All of the levels of thinking are interrelated and thus important to one another. This chapter will deal with how to ask for and evaluate those higher levels of thinking, with the goal of adding rigor to the classroom.

Analysis Level

Analysis is the level of thinking in which students actively look at a concept, break it down, and find the relationships among the parts. Analysis occurs when students have learned something and are then asked to look at it critically by "dissecting" the various parts that make up the whole. For example, when learning about the organs inside the body, the first level of thinking, knowledge, would require students to memorize the names of the organs—the heart, lungs, kidneys, etc. Then the students would need to understand the function of each organ—in other words, why do living things need these organs to survive? Next, they would have to be able to identify the organs in different life forms—do other animals such as dogs or frogs have lungs?

Now, we come to the analysis part. Once students know what the lungs look like and what they do, as well as what other types of living things need them, they should be able to look at a different species without lungs, say fish, and examine the differences between a fish and a human being. How are they alike? How are they different? For a fish, what serves the same purpose as the lungs? How does that work? Analysis involves taking a very close look and going beyond basic learned knowledge.

There are key words that can be used to generate analysis-level questions. Some of these words are:

analyze	compare	dissect	inspect	relationships	inference	classify
categorize	contrast	distinction	function	assumption	discover	
examine	survey	distinguish	theme	motive	conclusion	test for

One thing to be cautious about when using words associated with higher-level thinking is that if the information has already been taught and learned by students, the exercise becomes one of recalling information and negates the critical thinking component. In other words, if a science teacher had already taught his students the differences between human lungs and the gills of a fish, then asking them to identify the differences becomes a recall activity. A simple protocol to follow when trying to determine if the question is indeed at a higher level is to examine the definition of the level of thinking and determine if students are really demonstrating that. Using the question about the lungs of a human and the gills of a fish as an example, you could ask yourself:

Am I asking my students to examine and break information into parts by identifying motive or causes, making inferences, and finding evidence to support generalizations?

This is a description of analysis. If the answer to this question is "no," then using this same protocol with a lower-level of thinking could determine the answer. For example, you might ask yourself:

Am I asking my students to demonstrate an understanding of facts and ideas by comparing, translating, interpreting, or giving descriptions?

This is a description of the comprehension level of thinking. The complete protocol for determining the level of thinking can be found in the activity titled *At What Level Am I Asking My Students To Think?* found in the Blueprints section of this book.

Question stems for an analysis-level question may include:

What are the parts or features of...? How is _____ related to...?
Why, do you think? What is the theme...? What motive is there...?
Can you list the parts...? What inference can you make...?
What conclusions can you draw...? How would you classify...?
How would you categorize...? Can you identify the different parts...?
What is the relationship between...? What evidence can you find...?

Analysis-level questions can be asked in different formats. An example of a constructed response question asked at an analysis level for 5th grade reading would be:

How did the choice made by John when he decided to leave town affect what happened at the end of the story? What evidence from the text supports this?

The reason that this is an analysis-level question is because it requires students to examine the relationship between John's action and the end of the story. Again, it's important to note that this question will only require analysis if students have not learned this connection previously through classroom discussion or activities.

Analysis questions can also be asked using a multiple choice format. Consider the following example, which takes the constructed response question above, and puts it into a multiple choice format:

How did John's decision to leave town affect the plot of the story? Choose the best possible answer.

A. He was then able to graduate.

B. He then had more friends.

C. He was able to become mayor.

D. He was happy.

Graphic organizers may also be used to ask analysis questions. The same basic question about John's decision to leave town may be asked in a cause and effect chart like the one below:

Fill in the chart below listing the effects that John's actions had on the plot of the story.

John's Actions (Cause)	Effects on Plot
1.	1.
2.	2.

Some simple strategies you can use when asking analysis-level questions are:

- Ask the student to describe how two things are the same and/or different.

- Reading: *How are two of the characters alike? How are they different? What about two different versions of the same story? Or what about two different stories?*

- Math: Instead of asking students to work a problem, show two ways to solve the same problem. *What do they have in common? How are they different? What about two different algorithms. How are they alike? How are they different?*

- Social studies: Look at two important events in history. *How did they influence future events? What's the relationship between them? What conclusions can you draw?*

- Science: Examine two different theories or experiments. *What do they have in common? How are they different? How do they affect _____ today? Why do you think this is?*

- Ask students to look at several possible correct answers and determine which answer is the *best* answer.

- Ask students to classify things into groups and explain the reasons for their classification. This can be done with science concepts, short stories, math problems, and even a world crisis.

Analysis-level questions should provide you with information on whether or not students can take the information learned and dig even deeper to come up with completely new answers. This is a good way to increase the rigor in the classroom without having to generate new material—simply take the same material and increase the level of thinking. Although there may be several different "right" answers, you will be looking for the process of thinking rather than the product.

Synthesis Level

The fifth level of Bloom's is the synthesis level. Here students are asked to take something they have learned and do something different with it. This may mean taking it apart and putting it back together in a different form or taking one part of it and making something completely different.

Synthesis has some key words that may be used when generating questions:

build	compile	create	estimate	invent	plan	original	minimize
theorize	improve	change	compose	design	formulate	make up	
predict	modify	maximize	elaborate	combine	construct	develop	
imagine	originate	propose	suppose	adapt	relate	test	happen

Using these words to springboard into synthesis-level questions is helpful: *Predict what might happen. Change the ending. Invent a new way to do it.* Remember to be sure the question is actually asking students to synthesize information. For example, asking them to "formulate" the correct answer when working a mathematical equation is not synthesizing information, even though the word "formulate" is one of the key words.

These question stems may help you develop synthesis-level questions:

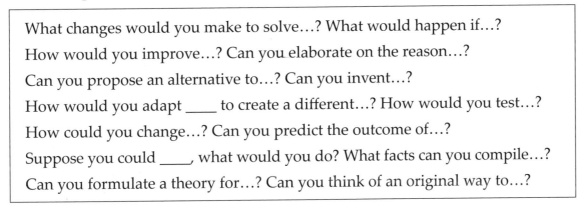

What changes would you make to solve…? What would happen if…?

How would you improve…? Can you elaborate on the reason…?

Can you propose an alternative to…? Can you invent…?

How would you adapt ____ to create a different…? How would you test…?

How could you change…? Can you predict the outcome of…?

Suppose you could ____, what would you do? What facts can you compile…?

Can you formulate a theory for…? Can you think of an original way to…?

Because synthesizing means putting information together in a different way, it makes sense that an effective format for this type of question is constructed response. Consider the following high school science question:

> **Taking information from the Periodic Table and the passage provided, propose something that would most likely be true about the Periodic Table. How could you change the Periodic Table to make it useful to students in the twenty-first century?**

The students are being asked first to analyze the information in the Periodic Table and the passage, then to make a proposition about the Periodic Table, which is doing something new with the information. Lastly, the students are being asked to change the Periodic Table to propose a different solution to a new situation.

Although constructed response questions, or ones in which students are being asked to write the answers, are a good format for synthesizing information, a multiple choice format can also be used to elicit this type of thinking. Take this example from a high school English exam:

> **If the setting of the book *To Kill a Mockingbird* had been in the north instead of in the south, how might that have changed the plot of the story? Choose the best answer.**
>
> A. Tom Robinson might have been sent to a different prison with better living conditions so he would not have felt the need to escape.

B. Boo Radley might have felt more comfortable living in the north, and consequently would not have been a recluse.

C. Tom Robinson might never have been convicted of rape based on the color of his skin since courts in the north may have been more objective.

D. Boo Radley may have been convicted of murdering Bob Ewell since nobody would be looking out for his anonymity.

To answer a synthesis question, students must be able to think at a more complex level than knowledge, comprehension, or application. The rigor of such a question is going to be much higher than one at a lower level. To answer the question above, not only do students need to know the plot of the book, but they also need to understand it, analyze it, and do something different with it.

Some simple strategies to introduce synthesis thinking include asking students to:

- Rewrite a different ending to a story.

- Work a math problem a different way.

- Tell how a world situation would be different if something different had occurred.

- Predict what would happen if something in a situation were to change.

- Play "what if?"

- List factors that might make something better or worse.

Synthesizing can be a great way to allow students to have fun with something while deepening their understanding. Being able to operate at a synthesis level of thinking truly insures that the learner understands the concept.

Evaluation Level

The final level of Bloom's Taxonomy is the evaluation level. This level asks students to form opinions and defend them based on a set of criteria. Many times teachers think students can say anything as an answer for this type of question and it will be correct. The trick to this level is the "criteria" part—it provides the parameters of the answer. Students need to adhere to the criteria to form and defend their opinions.

There are key words that can be used to generate these types of questions:

criticize	determine	judge	recommend	agree	opinion	support
prove	influence	choose	decide	dispute	justify	rule on	appraise
interpret	importance	disprove	perceive	conclude	defend	award
measure	rate	select	prioritize	assess	value	deduct	evaluate

These words can help formulate evaluation questions: *Which story do you think is the best one based on the lesson it teaches? Which math solution do you think makes the most sense and why? If you were the judge in this trial, how would you rule and why? Which scientific discovery do you think has had the most influence on the world today and why?*

There are also several question stems that can be used to generate evaluation-level questions:

Do you agree with _____?	Can you assess the value or importance of …
What is your opinion of…?	Why did (the character) choose…?
Would it be better if…?	How would you evaluate…?
Why was it better that…?	How would you justify…?
What would you select…?	How could you determine…?
What information would you use to support the view…?	
What data was used to make the conclusion…?	What do you like better…?

The purpose of evaluation-level questions is not only to determine if students can make judgments, but more importantly, how they defend their judgments. To defend their judgments students need to analyze their choices, and many times synthesize information in a different way. Look at the following mathematics problem:

The students in Mrs. Smith's class were given the following problem to solve:

$325 + 324 = $ _____ .

Heather solved the problem the following way:

$$\begin{array}{r} 325 \\ +\ 324 \\ \hline 649 \end{array}$$

Chad solved the problem this way:

" $300 + 300 = 600$, and $25 + 25 = 50$, so $25 + 24$ would equal 49, so the answer is 649."

Which of the two ways (Heather's or Chad's) do you think is the easier way to solve the problem? Explain your answer.

To answer this question correctly the students need to analyze the two choices, make their judgments, and defend their opinions based on the criterion: which is the easiest way to solve the problem?

When adding rigor to any classroom, keep in mind that higher-level questions need not be reserved for older students. The following question can be given to very young children when asking them to evaluate:

Which book is your favorite and why?

Or the question could be asked this way:

Which book is your favorite ? What was the best part of the book?

Evaluation questions can apply easily to every subject area from history to art to physical education, where students could be asked which sport they would most like to excel at and why. In art class, students could be asked which painter they think had the most influence on the Impressionist movement and why. Again, remember the justification of the opinion is equally as important as, if not more important than, the opinion itself.

Some easy strategies to use when moving students to evaluate information are to have them:

- Fill out interest inventories—they are full of evaluation-level questions.
- Look at a world event and defend the actions of opposing sides of the argument.
- Look at one solution to a math problem and tell if it is the easiest way to solve the problem and why.
- Discuss which character in a story they most identify with and why.
- Determine which school rule they would most like to change and why.

Although the evaluation level of Bloom's Taxonomy is the highest, it is actually one of the easier and most pleasurable levels for students to demonstrate. Many teachers are familiar with the evaluation level, which makes it very "user friendly." Evaluation is a good way to begin to add rigor to the classroom without even making the students aware of it.

The "Critical" Part of Writing Higher-Level Questions

The three higher levels of thinking—*analysis, synthesis,* and *evaluation*—can be assessed using different question formats. Although it seems open-ended constructed response questions would be easiest, you can format multiple choice questions as well when assessing student competency in the critical, higher levels of thinking. It's important to consider the type of thinking students are being asked to use when formulating questions—when asking them to *analyze* something, students need to break information apart to determine relationships; to *synthesize* information, they need to compile that information together in a different way to come up with a new solution; and to *evaluate* something, students need to present an opinion based on a set of criteria and support their opinions.

It's also important to remember that simply using the key words or question stems provided does not mean the question is at a higher level. If you ask students to *determine* the main character of a story, you are not requiring them to evaluate anything—even though the word *determine* is often used in evaluation questions. In that case, students are simply recalling information. Likewise, if the information has been taught to students previously, it negates the higher-level component of the question. An example of this would be a question on a test that asks students to argue both the pros and cons of entering the Vietnam War, after their social studies class had already discussed the pros and cons of that war. The students would only be providing information that had already been taught.

Another important component of questioning to achieve higher-level thinking lies in the answers students provide and how to evaluate those answers. Explanations and examples of these components will be provided in Chapter 7, where we address analyzing the data from higher-level questions.

Perhaps the most crucial aspect of adding rigor to the classroom is integrating higher-level critical thinking questions into the daily classroom setting. Starting out, these types of questions can be added informally, for example, as part of a discussion in class. As you progress in your own understanding of critical thinking, and as you provide your students with more experience in thinking at higher levels, you will want to assess whether or not they are becoming proficient in these levels. The next chapter will provide information about how to include questions in formative assessments so you have the data necessary to show that you are indeed increasing the rigor in relation to critical thinking in your curriculum.

6
Writing Formative Assessments with Critical Thinking Questions

If you don't change assessment, nothing changes.

Bernice McCarthy

What is a Formative Assessment?

A formative assessment occurs with instruction and provides specific feedback to teachers and students for the purpose of guiding teaching toward improved learning (McTighe and O'Connor, 2005). Formative assessments can be informal, as in observation or oral questioning, or they can be formal, as is the case with short-cycle assessments. The following figure shows examples of both:

Formal Formative Assessments	Informal Formative Assessments
• Common Short-Cycle Assessments	• Observation
• Performance Assessments	• Oral Questioning
• Homework Assignments	• Student-Teacher Conferences
• Flashcards	• Conversations with Other Teachers
• Exit Cards	• Conversations with Parents
• Surveys	• Student-Led Conferences

You may notice that several of the assessments in the formal column could also be summative assessments. A summative assessment is when you assess with the purpose of giving a grade without the opportunity for improvement or further understanding. When looking at formative versus summative assessment, the important thing is the intent or purpose for which it's being used.

The main thing to remember about formative assessment is that it provides information to guide instruction. It's the so-called roadmap that lets you know if the trip is going to be rocky with lots of peaks and valleys, or if it's going to be a smooth ride. It's important to know the terrain ahead so you can best prepare; you don't want to run into a rocky road without having equipped yourself with a good pair of shocks or hit a hilly stretch without having first checked the brakes. Similarly, you don't want to teach things students already know or assume things they don't know—you want to give your students the smoothest ride possible.

That's why adding critical thinking questions to formative assessments is essential. As teachers, we should constantly and consistently be assessing what we teach. Otherwise how will we know whether our students have learned what has been taught? If we consciously *assess* critical thinking skills, it only makes sense we'll spend the appropriate amount of time *teaching* critical thinking skills. As a result, teaching critical thinking skills becomes very intentional. This is a great example of the backwards buildings model of Grant Wiggins and Jay McTighe (Wiggins and McTighe, 1998), where the teacher develops the assessment ahead of time and "builds" instruction backwards from it. In this way, you can be assured that you are adding rigor to your instruction and that students are learning at these higher levels.

The question then becomes, how do you add critical thinking components to your formative assessments? We'll explore this question by looking at a specific type of formative assessment—short-cycle assessments—and how adding critical thinking questions will allow you to make sure students have learned the critical thinking skills you have taught.

The SCORE Process

An easy process to use when developing formative short-cycle assessments is one called the SCORE process outlined in the book, *Short-Cycle Assessment: Improving Student Achievement Through Formative Assessment* (Lang, Stanley, and Moore, 2008). SCORE stands for:

S   Short

C   Cycle Assessments

O   Organized for

R   Results and

E   Expectations

SCORE is a process that takes teachers step-by-step through the creation of their own short-cycle assessments. There are six main steps involved in the SCORE process:

1. Understanding the State Standards and State Assessments
2. Developing a Pacing Guide
3. Developing an Assessment
4. Administrating the Assessment
5. Analyzing the Data from the Assessment
6. Making Instructional Improvements Based on the Data

To understand how to integrate higher-level critical thinking questions into a formative short-cycle assessment, it's imperative that you understand the components of the SCORE process. This chapter will take you through the first four steps of the SCORE process. Along the way we'll describe how the critical thinking component fits into the mix.

Step 1: Understanding the State Standards and State Assessments

Prior to developing any kind of formative assessment, you must first understand what students need to learn. In this day of standards-based learning, most subject areas and grade levels are tied to academic content standards developed at either the state or national level. Some of these standards are assessed on state tests, while others are subject to end-of-course exams. Others are not assessed in an official capacity; yet even if the subject you teach doesn't have a high-stakes state test, it's highly probable that your students will be required to take one in another subject. One rationale for creating formative short-cycle assessments is that they allow you to know what students have learned in your class throughout the learning experience in a way that is similar to the state test. This will help to guide your instruction and create a better learning environment for the standards you're required to teach. Another rationale for formative short-cycle assessments is that, through the development of the questions, you'll learn exactly what the standards mean, and at what levels they should be taught.

There are a number of ways to go about understanding the standards for your subject area. A couple of simple strategies are found in the Blueprints section of this book, including making an *I Can...* list or filling out a *How I Would Instruct It/How I Would Assess It* chart. As you begin to implement critical thinking into your formative assessments, you'll continue to deepen your understanding of the standards—the so-called nucleus of the process.

Another important component to developing a formative short-cycle assessment with higher-level thinking questions, and the second part of Step 1 in the SCORE process, is understanding the state assessment and how the standards are being presented. Whether your students take a state achievement test, an end-of-course exam (otherwise known as an exit exam), an AP test, or even an SAT or ACT exam, you'll need to analyze the format of the assessment. While each test is unique, there are certain commonalities among the types of questions each one uses. For the most part, these tests use one of the following types of questions: multiple choice, constructed response, response grid, or writing prompts.

The important thing to consider when developing an assessment aligned to the academic content standards is to use the same format the students will see on the high-stakes test. For example, the ACT and SAT exams used to be only multiple choice; therefore it would have made sense to include these types of questions on a short-cycle assessment in subject areas that prepare students for these tests. Recently, however, these two exams have added constructed response questions as well as writing prompts—so, in developing a formative short-cycle assessment designed to prepare students for the ACT or SAT, it would make sense to include all three types. Likewise, if your state test doesn't have response grid questions (usually reserved for math and science problems), it wouldn't make sense to put these on your short-cycle assessment. If your state test does have response grid questions, you would want to include them on your own assessments.

The rationale for understanding the state assessments is to know what type of question format to include in your own formative short-cycle assessment. To break down the amount of multiple choice or constructed response questions on your state test, we recommend you use the *Questions Conversion Chart* found in the Blueprints section of this book. This will help in determining how many different question types to include on your short-cycle assessments.

An important part of the first step in the SCORE process—Understanding the State Standards and State Assessments—is understanding the level of the content or the level of the standards. When working to add critical thinking questions to a formative short-cycle assessment, you need to know the level of thinking for each academic content standard. Those levels are varied. Some states are writing their standards so that they directly assess students in higher-level thinking skills. Take for instance this standard from the New York State Learning Standards under Science–Living Environment:

> **Standard 3.1—Use various methods of representing and organizing observations (e.g., diagrams, tables, charts, graphs, equations, matrices) and insightfully interpret the organized data.**

This doesn't seem like the typical use of graphs and charts. This standard calls for students to "insightfully interpret"—most definitely a higher level of thinking.

Or what about this standard from the Texas Essential Knowledge and Skills (TEKS) with regard to English:

> **Analyze characters, including their traits, feelings, relationships and changes.**

You'd think this is something seniors in an AP English course would be doing, but this standard is for 1st to 3rd graders. Obviously higher-level thinking is expected in Texas even at a very early age.

Finally, look at this standard from the Ohio Standards in the subject of social studies:

> Compare direct and representative democracy using examples of ancient Athens, the Roman republic and the United States today.

In this example students are asked to compare several periods of time, not to simply repeat back facts. Through this comparison, connections and higher-level thinking clearly are occurring.

Even if your state standards are written to require only lower-level thinking from students, it behooves you to include higher-level, critical thinking questions throughout your assessments. After all, it's better for students who are being assessed on a particular standard to actually be able to analyze that standard. Students' ability to answer questions at a higher level of thinking shows a deeper understanding that will more likely lead to enduring learning. The inclusion of these critical thinking questions will increase the rigor of your class and prepare students for work and life—where they will most likely have to make critical thinking decisions on a day-to-day basis.

So, how can you be sure you're addressing the standards and asking questions at the higher level of thinking their content suggests? A simple way to determine the level of a standard is by using the *Taxonomy Table* (a blank one is provided in the Blueprints section of this book). In a Taxonomy Table each standard is analyzed to determine the level of Bloom's at which it's set. The first step in doing this is to study each verb in the standard, deciding the level of Bloom's at which it falls. For example, if a standard states...

Identify the characters and setting in a story.

...we would highlight the verb *identify*. If the standard reads...

Analyze how the setting influences the plot of a story.

...we would highlight the verb *analyze.*

It doesn't end here, however. We need to discuss and decide at which level of Bloom's the standard is set. In these two cases, the verbs lead to a fairly simple conclusion: The first standard's verb is *identify* so that would be classified as a knowledge-level standard. The second standard's verb is *analyze* so that would be classified as an analysis-level standard. But sometimes the standard isn't that obvious. Look at the following standard:

Examine an author's implicit and explicit philosophical assumptions and beliefs about a subject.

Because the verb *examine* isn't one of the six labeled levels of Bloom's Taxonomy, it takes some thinking to figure out that students are being asked to analyze the author's assumptions and beliefs. That puts this standard at the analysis level. Another important point to consider is that just because the verb is used in the standard doesn't mean the standard is actually at that level of Bloom's. Consider this standard:

Determine the meaning of unknown words using a dictionary.

By using only the key words associated with Bloom's Taxonomy, *determine* would indicate that this standard is classified as being at the evaluation level. Upon examining the type of thinking students are being asked to use, it's clear they're not making a judgment based on a set of criteria, but rather solving problems in new situations (the unknown word) by applying acquired techniques (using the dictionary). That places this standard at the application level. The point here is that the type of thinking and the actual verb need to be examined when determining levels of thinking.

The next step in the Taxonomy Table activity is to place each standard in the chart to create a clear visual representation of where that standard falls. For example, if the standard is written at an analysis level, it would be placed in that column on the chart. See the example below.

Partial Taxonomy Table

Subject/Grade:Rdg.Gr.3 Descriptor of Standard	Knowledge	Comprehension	Application	Analysis	Synthesis	Evaluation
Acquisition of Vocabulary	Obj. # 1 Obj. # 5	Obj. # 2 Obj. # 3 Obj. # 6	Obj. # 4			
Reading Processes		Obj. # 1 Obj. # 3 Obj. # 4	Obj. # 2 Obj. # 5 Obj. # 6	Obj. # 8 Obj. # 10		Obj. # 7 Obj. # 9
Literary Text				Obj. # 2 Obj. # 3	Obj. # 1	Obj. # 4 Obj. # 5

For an example of a *Completed Taxonomy Table*, refer to the Blueprints section.

Step 2: Developing a Pacing Guide

Once you understand the importance of determining the level for each standard, it's time to put it all together into a *Pacing Guide* (a blank one is provided in the Blueprints Section). Developing a Pacing Guide is the second step in the SCORE process. A Pacing Guide is simply a sorting tool used to plan when to assess a particular standard during the school year. When developing a short-cycle assessment, you need to have a way to divide the standards so that all of them can be assessed. The SCORE process uses a Pacing Guide to separate the standards.

When developing a Pacing Guide, there are several important things to consider. The following are several considerations to think about as you work through placing the standards into a Pacing Guide.

- Although you might teach that skill all the time, you may only assess the skill a handful of times. *The Pacing Guide helps you decide when to assess.*

- Think about when you want the **information** on whether or not the student has mastered the skill, or what progress the student has made toward mastery.

- Think about when you would become **concerned** if the student could not do the skill described in the standard. You should place the standard on the Pacing Guide before this happens.

- Think about when you would provide **intervention** with regard to the standard.

- If the standard has several skills involved, you may **break apart** the standard into pieces.

- You may put the standard in **more than one** grading period.

A partially completed Pacing Guide is shown below. As you can see, it's a simple matter of deciding which standards to assess in which time segment.

Partial Pacing Guide

Grading Period 1	*Grading Period 2*	*Grading Period 3*	*Grading Period 4*
Standards	*Standards*	*Standards*	*Standards*
2-1	2-2	2-6	2-7
2-3	2-4	3-1	3-1
2-5	3-1	3-6	3-8b
3-1	3-2	3-8a	4-6
3-3	3-4	4-4	4-7
4-2	3-5	4-5	5-2
5-1	4-1	5-3	5-5
	4-3	5-4	5-6

A combination of a Pacing Guide and a Taxonomy Table is a *Leveled Pacing Guide* (a blank one can be found in the Blueprints section). In essence, a Leveled Pacing Guide is one where you determine the level of Bloom's at the same time you decide on the placement of the standard. Below is an example of a 5th grade reading (Reading Applications: Literary Text) Leveled Pacing Guide. The standards are provided in list form first, with the actual Leveled Pacing Guide including only the numbers following that. It is important to note that a list of the standards should always be included with a Pacing Guide or a Leveled Pacing Guide. Otherwise, all you have is a chart with a lot of numbers!

Standard # 1: Describe the thoughts, words, and interactions of characters.

Standard # 2: Analyze the influence of setting on the selection.

Standard # 3: Identify the main incidents of a plot sequence, identifying the major conflict and its resolution.

Standard # 4: Identify the speaker and recognize the difference between first- and third-person narration.

Standard # 5: Determine the theme and whether it is implied or stated directly.

Standard # 6: Identify and explain the defining characteristics of literary forms and genres, including poetry, drama, fables, fantasies, chapter books, fiction, and non-fiction.

Standard # 7: Explain how an author's choice of words appeals to the senses and suggests mood.

Standard # 8: Identify figurative language in literary works, including idioms, similes and metaphors.

Notice that in standard #6, the verbs are *identify* and *explain*. When the standard is being asked at two different levels (knowledge and comprehension), you may either place the standard in the higher level or place it in both the higher and lower level—never just the lower level. Continue doing this for all the standards for your subject area. This activity will not only deepen a teacher's understanding of the standards, but will also help determine the questions to use in assessing the higher-level standards on a formative assessment.

Grade 5 Leveled Pacing Guide

Level	Grading Period 1	Grading Period 2	Grading Period 3	Grading Period 4
Knowledge	#6 (Identify)	# 4	# 3 #8	
Comprehension	# 1	# 6 (Explain)		# 7
Application				
Analysis				# 2
Synthesis				
Evaluation		# 5		

Step 3: Developing an Assessment

Having learned how to write questions in the last two chapters, and combining that with the information you gained from leveling and sorting your academic content standards, you're now ready to put everything together into a short-cycle assessment. This leads us to the third step in the SCORE process—developing an assessment. Developing an assessment can be done by writing your own questions, or by selecting questions that already exist. We strongly recommend writing the questions for the simple reason that the more practice you have in writing higher-level critical thinking questions, the more comfortable you will become in asking them in your day-to-day instruction. We do realize, however, that there are a lot of high-quality questions that have already been written, and teachers do not always have the time to sit down and write their own questions. If you do select published questions, make sure they're assessing the content of the standard as well as the level at which the standard is written. If you are not sure which route to take—writing your own questions, or using published questions—consider this: are students learning more by copying the answer out of the book or by coming up with an answer on their own? If your goal is to learn how to ask higher-level questions with confidence, the best route would be to write your own questions.

Sometimes it helps to look at already established questions before writing your own. This will give you an idea of what they should look like and inspire you to create better questions. To provide this inspiration, we've put together a list of questions for the five core content areas, using various standards (see *Sample Questions* in the Blueprints section). These questions can be used to help you better understand what questions at different levels look like. You can also "tweak" these questions if you choose to use them in your instruction or on your assessment.

If you decide to go with already published questions, another thing to keep in mind is the format. Remember, you want to use the format of your state test as much as possible; therefore you need to choose your questions according to that format. If you find a true/false question that you think correctly assesses the level, you can always rewrite it into a multiple choice or constructed response question. This tweaking may have to be done for the question to fit into the format of your short-cycle assessment. For instance, look at the question below:

> **We use words in English that come from other cultures. In the selections the word "colossus" is used to describe two statues. What other object can be described as a colossus?**
>
> A. The size of a football field.
>
> B. The size of our school.
>
> C. The size of a school bus.
>
> D. The size of the Grand Canyon.

This multiple choice question can easily be rewritten as a constructed response question by eliminating the answer choices and adding the directive, "explain your answer" to the end. Thus, the multiple choice question becomes the following constructed response question:

> **We use words in English that come from other cultures. In the selections the word "colossus" is used to describe two statues. What other object can be described as a colossus? Explain your answer.**

In summary, whether you decide to write your own questions for a formative short-cycle assessment or find already published questions, there are some common guidelines to follow as described in the SCORE process:

- The number of questions should be from 15 to 25. The questions need to fairly assess the standard.

- The assessment should use the same language/vocabulary as the high-stakes test.

- The assessment should use the same format as the high-stakes test.

- The assessment should use the same distribution of questions as the high-stakes test.

This is just a partial list of guidelines. A complete *Short-Cycle Assessment Checklist* can be found in the Blueprints section.

Step 4: Administering the Assessment

Step four of the SCORE process concerns the administration of the assessment. To get the biggest bang for your buck you should have the students take the short-cycle assessment in the same type of "test setting" that they will use for the high-stakes test. This will allow the students to become more familiar with the testing environment and ultimately lead to a higher level of comfort.

Answers to Critical Thinking Questions—What to Look For

As you are grading your formative short-cycle assessments following administration, you have to know what to look for to determine competency in critical thinking skills. If you want affirmation that your students have indeed performed at a higher level of thinking, go back to the original descriptors of each type of thinking and compare that with your Leveled Pacing Guide. For example, if the standard is a 7th grade math standard that states…

> **Construct opposing arguments based on analysis of the same data, using different graphical representations.**

…and you have determined it to be at a synthesis level because it requires students to compile information in a different way by combining elements in a new pattern or proposing alternative solutions, the answers students provide should show they are indeed putting the information together in a way that's different.

We've provided an easy-to-use tool, titled *Critical Thinking Flowchart* for evaluating whether or not critical thinking is being demonstrated by students. You can find this tool in the Blueprints section. We will also provide more information on creating rubrics for higher-level thinking questions, and how to grade those questions, in the next chapter. Knowing what to look for in higher-level thinking answers is just as important as knowing how to ask higher-level thinking questions.

The "Critical" Part of Writing Formative Assessments with Critical Thinking Questions

Once you understand how to write critical thinking questions, you're ready to add these to your formative assessments. This can be done in either informal formative assessments (e.g., oral questioning), or formal formative assessments (e.g., short-cycle assessments). Prior to creating short-cycle formative assessments, it's important to understand the content area standards as well as the state or national exam. The questions will need to be asked at the level of the standard and in the same format as the test they are emulating. The choice of which standards to assess comes from the creation of a Pacing Guide, which "sorts" the standards into shorter time frames throughout the school year. When a Pacing Guide is a Leveled Pacing Guide, it serves the function of coding the standards according to the level of Bloom's Taxonomy into which they fall. In this way, it's easy to see which standards need to have questions for which grading period, as well as the level of Bloom's at which the questions need to be asked.

When creating formative short-cycle assessments, either teacher-developed questions or published questions may be used, although teacher-developed will better help you learn to be comfortable with higher-level questioning. The most important thing to consider is whether the questions are adequately and fairly assessing the standards.

One last "critical" part to consider when developing formative assessments— even if the questions you place on your assessments are at a "higher level" than your standards and the state test, they will actually benefit your students by requiring them to think and perform at a critical thinking level. This is what raising the level of rigor in your classroom is all about. What many employers today are indicating in the workplace is that prospective entry-level employees don't know how to think. Teaching students how to think at a higher level and assessing them at that level is truly going a long way toward solving the "thinking problem."

7

Analyzing the Data from Critical Thinking Questions: What Does It All Mean?

Thought once awakened does not again slumber.

Thomas Carlyle

Step 5: Analyzing the Data from the Assessment

Following the administration and grading of the assessment, you will have all kinds of data. Now what? What you do or do not do with the data is the most important step in the SCORE process. One thing we know is that the educational world is inundated with data. We have data from nationally standardized tests, state achievement tests, classroom diagnostic tests, and summative classroom assessments just to name a few. In addition, we have performance assessments and anecdotal records to review. This leads us to several essential questions:

- What are the important things to consider when looking at data for critical thinking questions?

- How can we know if our students have truly learned to think at a higher level?

- How can we show that we're providing the rigor necessary for our students to succeed in today's world?

Of course the best way to know that your students are adept at critical thinking is by providing modeling and practice on a consistent basis. Constantly asking higher-level questions, both orally and on written assignments, is a good way to start. What we sometimes forget is that it's important to actually teach students how to think at the higher levels. Simply providing the questions and then assigning them a grade won't have much effect if the students aren't provided with feedback on how to improve.

The rest of this chapter will focus on the fifth step of the SCORE process—Analyzing the Data from the Assessment. We'll provide you with information about how to look at the data, and how to know if your students have actually mastered higher-level thinking. Then, in Chapter 8, we'll show you what to do if mastery has not occurred.

Grading the Critical Thinking Questions in Formative Assessments

One of the most important steps in analyzing data actually occurs before you have it; that would be making sure the data you get is valid. If you receive data that's wrong or measures something other than what you intended, your analysis will also be incorrect. That's why it is extremely important to grade the formative assessment accurately to ensure valid data.

Constructed response higher-level thinking questions may be less difficult to write than multiple choice, but the grading of them in some cases is more challenging. The first thing to consider is whether or not answers are demonstrating the level of thinking that's being assessed. For example, if the question is assessing the synthesis level, students should be compiling information together in a different way. Because critical thinking questions can have more than one correct answer, it is imperative that the answer key be as complete and detailed as possible. This is especially true if your assessment is a common one that other teachers are using. Asking for a complete list of answer possibilities for a higher-level, constructed response question is a bit unrealistic. However, it can be argued that there are definitive boundaries within which the correct answer lies.

For example, let's say a student is asked to write a different ending to the story *Jack and the Beanstalk* and his answer is an ending to *Little Red Riding Hood*, then his answer would be incorrect. Likewise, a student may be asked to give an opinion about something using certain criteria and support his opinion by giving textual evidence. If the student doesn't follow the criteria when stating his opinion, or if he fails to give textual evidence, the answer would again be considered incorrect.

The rule of thumb for your answer key should be, "Could someone not teaching my particular class use this answer key to grade the assessment?" Here are some possibilities for making a good answer key for a critical thinking constructed response question:

1. Use a rubric.
2. Give as many plausible answers as you can think of.
3. Include an incorrect example.
4. Provide anchor answers.

If you and your colleagues determine that "Because I like it" is an incorrect answer, then put that in the answer key. Determine anchor answers—student responses you consider to be "exemplary"—and attach them to the answer key as examples of mastery. An example of how to make up an anchor answer, along with a specific example of an anchor answer can be found in the blueprint titled *Developing Answer Rubrics for Critical Thinking Questions*. In addition to anchor answers, make up answer-specific rubrics for each of the questions. Brainstorm possible answers and provide as many as you can. Writing rubrics for answers in an answer key is different than writing rubrics that will serve as general compass points for a specific piece of writing. For an answer key, each question will need a rubric, and that rubric will deal specifically with the content of the question. For an example of how to come up with an answer-specific rubric, refer again to the blueprint *Developing Answer Rubrics for Critical Thinking Questions*.

One last thing to consider when making an answer key for constructed response higher-level questions is to never, ever use the phrases "Answers will vary" or "Accept reasonable answers." These serve to muddy the waters and add confusion and doubt to the validity of the assessment. A detailed answer key is one of the most important aspects of a valid test. An example of a *Detailed Answer Key* has been provided for you in the Blueprints section at the end of this book. This detailed Answer Key should serve as an example for you as you strive to make your own answer key as clear as possible.

Compiling the Data

The simplest way of looking at any kind of data is to put it into chart form. Because most of us are visual learners, representing the information visually helps us see the big picture. When compiling the data you can choose to include all of the questions on the formative assessment, or you can choose to include only the critical thinking questions.

You do need, however, to separate the lower-level from the higher-level thinking questions. For our purposes in this chapter we will deal with the critical thinking data only.

The first step in compiling the data is to identify the questions in your formative assessment that assess critical thinking skills. This should be fairly easy if you've already identified the standards involving critical thinking and chosen higher-level questions to assess them. How you set up the chart is your choice; one way is provided in the example on the facing page:

Critical Thinking Data Chart

Student Name	#3 St. 4 Syn	#5 St. 5 Anly	#8 St. 7 Anly	#9 St. 10 Eval	#11 St. 4 Syn	#13 St. 4 Syn	#15 St. 10 Eval	#16 St. 7 Anly	#18 St. 4 Syn	#20 St. 5 Anly	Total Pts.	%
Beth	2	0	1	2	3	1	0	1	0	2	12/17	71%
John	1	0	1	1	2	1	1	1	1	2	11/17	65%
Heather	1	0	1	1	2	1	1	1	0	2	10/17	59%
Matt	0	0	1	1	1	1	1	1	1	1	8/17	47%
Josh	1	0	1	1	1	1	0	1	0	2	8/17	47%
Taylor	2	0	1	0	2	2	0	1	1	1	10/17	59%
Shelly	1	1	0	1	3	2	1	1	0	1	11/17	65%
Amy	2	1	0	2	4	1	1	1	1	2	15/17	88%
Nick	1	1	1	2	3	2	0	1	0	2	13/17	76%
Dave	2	1	1	1	4	1	0	1	1	2	14/17	82%
Ron	1	1	1	2	3	1	1	1	0	2	13/17	76%
Jill	2	0	1	1	3	1	1	1	1	2	13/17	76%
Ann	2	0	1	2	3	1	1	1	0	2	13/17	76%
Darin	1	0	1	2	4	2	0	1	1	2	14/17	82%
Points Earned	19	5	12	19	38	18	8	14	7	25		
Possible Points	28	14	14	28	56	28	14	14	14	28		
Ques. %	68%	36%	86%	68%	68%	64%	57%	100%	50%	89%		

Here are the steps for creating this particular chart:

1. Write the number at the top of the chart in the first row.
2. Underneath that write the standard.
3. Identify the level of thinking the question is assessing (i.e., synthesis, analysis, or evaluation).
4. Fill out the score each student earned for each of the questions.
5. In the right hand column of the chart, total the point value and the percentage.
6. At the bottom of the chart, tabulate the points earned for each question.
7. Divide that number by the total of points possible to find the correct percentage for each of the questions.

We have provided a blank template titled *Critical Thinking Data Chart* in the Blueprints section to help you compile your critical thinking data.

Analyzing the Data

Once you've completed the data chart you are ready to analyze the results of the formative assessment. You'll want to make a Class Profile Graph for this. This graph will determine whether you need to go back and reteach the entire class because they don't "get it" or if you simply need to focus on a couple of individuals. The graph can be created electronically or can be handwritten. To make a graph of this type:

1. Write each student's name in the *x* axis
2. Write the percentage of 0–100% in the *y* axis
3. Color in the overall percentage each student scored—that is to say, the whole percentage of all of the critical thinking questions combined.

An example of a Class Profile Graph is shown on the facing page, and there is a blank *Class Profile Graph for Critical Thinking Questions* template located in the Blueprints section of this book for your convenience. The types of questions you'd want to ask when looking at a graph like this include:

- What was the overall mean of the class? (You find this by adding up each student's percentage and dividing that by the total number of students.)
- Is the overall percentage acceptable?
- Which students did very well on the critical thinking questions?
- Which students performed poorly?
- Were any students significantly different than the others? Were they below or above the others?

Class Profile Graph

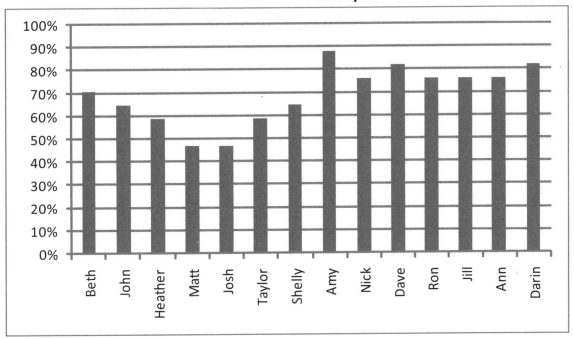

An important thing to look for in the Class Profile Graph is the mean. If most of your students fall within a few percentage points of each other, then the students have learned what you've taught them. If some are significantly different, then they either haven't learned what has been taught or are performing beyond what was taught. Exactly what you determine to be acceptable as far as the mean is up to you. Many go with 75%; others feel that the mastery rate should be 80% or higher. If you're trying to raise the level of rigor in your classroom, you'll want to go with the 80% or higher. Likewise, if you've been working with a group just being introduced to a concept you might accept lower numbers. We recommend you look for consistent scores over time above 75%, which means your students are successful in answering critical thinking questions three-fourths of the time. If all of your students score at or near a percentage you would consider to be too low, you might want to ask what you need to do to improve your expertise in teaching critical thinking skills.

Once you have the overall picture of how students are doing, disaggregate the data further and examine how the students are performing in each area of critical thinking. For instance, are they getting the analysis questions but not performing so well on the synthesis questions? The chart on the next page is a "sorting tool" that will help determine in which areas of critical thinking each student has achieved proficiency, and in which areas they still need work.

This chart can be used to determine which students need further practice/ instruction, similarly identifying which levels of critical thinking to focus on. For your convenience, we have provided a blank sorting chart titled *Proficiency on Critical Thinking Items Chart* in the Blueprints section.

Sorting Chart

Student's Name	Analysis		Synthesis		Evaluation	
	Yes	No	Yes	No	Yes	No
Beth	|||			||	||				
John	|||					|||				
Heather	|||				||||				
Matt	||	||				|||				
Josh	|||				||||			||
Taylor	||	||	|||					||
Shelly	||	||	||						
Amy	|||			|||			||	
Nick	||||		||							
Dave	|||		|||					||
Ron	||||				|||	||	
Jill	|||		|||						
Ann	|||		||	||	||	
Darin	|||		|||						

Finally, for instructional purposes, it's important to analyze how the class performed as a whole on the different critical thinking items. This will indicate what particular areas of critical thinking you may need to focus on in the classroom. It could also indicate any problems that exist within the questions on the assessment. You'll need to take the data from your data chart and make an Item Analysis Graph. A sample Item Analysis Graph is shown on the facing page.

Steps to creating this graph are:

1. Write the question numbers, standards, and levels of thinking on the *x* axis.

2. Write the percentages from 0 to 100 on the *y* axis.

3. From your data chart, add up the number of points actually scored by all of the students for each question. You can do this by simply counting the scores in each column.

4. Take that number and divide it by the total number of points possible to get a percentage.

For this particular class the students scored 70% on question number 15. That means that the class as a whole scored 70 out of 100 percent on a question that was at an evaluation level. Instructionally, this indicates that while 70% is a good score, 30% of the students did not attain mastery on that question. This may mean that the class would benefit from some additional instruction or practice in the area of evaluating information. In addition to the sample shown on the facing page, we've provided a blank *Critical Thinking Item Analysis Graph* in the Blueprints section.

Item Analysis Graph

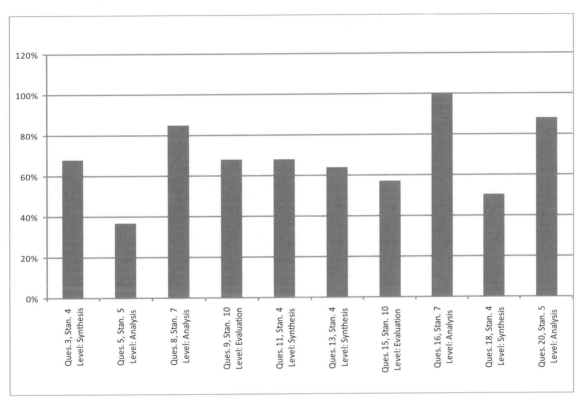

When analyzing data, there are several important things to consider. The following chart shows the important things you need to ask yourself or look for as you study the data with regard to critical thinking skills.

What to Look For
• Data that is going to directly affect instruction for increased student achievement.
• Results that do not make sense.
• Strengths and improvements to be made as a teacher.
• Data that will help you learn from others and promote collaboration.
• Trends in the data.
• The specific types of critical thinking skills on which your students did well.
• The specific types of critical thinking skills on which your students did poorly.

In addition, there are different questions you'll want to ask yourself when analyzing the data. Some of these questions include:

- How much time did you spend teaching the different critical thinking skills?

- How did you instruct the students with regard to these skills?

- Were there any extenuating circumstances that could impact the data—calamity days, poor attendance, personal issues in a student's life, etc.?

- Were there any differences in the format of the questions with regard to performance; e.g., did the students score better on the multiple choice questions or on the constructed response questions? What does this mean?

This represents a partial list of questions to ask when analyzing data. A more complete list is in the Blueprints section and is titled *Questions to Ask When Analyzing Data with Regard to Critical Thinking Skills.*

The ultimate question becomes what to do if only a few students are not getting the critical thinking questions. Do you reteach the entire class? If you do that, might some students become bored? That's where differentiated instruction comes into play. We'll discuss differentiated instruction in the next chapter.

The "Critical" Part of Analyzing the Data from Critical Thinking Questions

Part of analyzing data from formative assessments that contain critical thinking questions lies in scoring the constructed response items. You need to be able to define the parameters within which critical thinking is taking place. The first criteria in the scoring should be whether or not the answer displays the type of thinking being assessed. Then, as many examples as possible should be included in the answer key. If possible, include unacceptable answers—what not to do. Sometimes outlining the types of answers is helpful. Finally, scoring rubrics and anchor answers should become important components of an answer key.

After scoring a formative assessment, the data must be compiled. The easiest way to do this is by putting the data into a chart, then generating different graphs according to your needs. Some of these might include classroom profile graphs and item analysis graphs. When analyzing the data, different questions should be asked—and all of the questions should be connected to student achievement with regard to critical thinking skills.

One last thing to remember: most times an assessment, whether formal or informal, is a snapshot. Don't assume that just because students score poorly on a question in which they are to analyze information they lack analysis skills. Similarly, one correct question may not mean students have mastered that level of thinking. When looking at data, you need to study trends over time as well as other student scores. If a majority of your students score poorly on the analysis questions, you may need to look at how the skill of analyzing was instructed.

Analyzing data sometimes means asking the hard questions—not only of your students but also of yourself. It's only by becoming proficient in analyzing data for critical thinking that you will truly be able to provide perhaps the most important component of rigor—the evidence of learning.

8

Instructional Strategies to Develop Critical Thinking Skills in the Classroom

Insanity is doing the same things over and over again and expecting different results.

Albert Einstein

You Have the Data, Now What?

Now that you've analyzed the data on your students' ability to answer higher-level critical thinking questions, what do you do with that information? That leads us to step six of the SCORE process—Making Instructional Improvements Based on the Data. You probably came up with several instructional implications, and most of you no doubt included, "I need to teach my students how to think at a higher, critical thinking level." That is simple enough to say. The difficult part is *how* to teach those skills.

Step 6: Making Instructional Improvements Based on the Data

As we stated in the last chapter, analyzing the data from your formative short-cycle assessment is perhaps the most important step in the SCORE process. With that said, equal value has to be placed on what you do *after* you have analyzed the data. Analysis without action will not change anything in the classroom. So, what do you do now? We'll explore that question as we discuss specific instructional strategies that can be employed following analysis of the data. First, however, we want to talk about some key factors that influence the teaching of critical thinking skills in the classroom.

Factors Influencing the Teaching of Critical Thinking Skills

Time *seems* to be the biggest deterrent to teaching critical thinking skills. "If we only had a little more time" is the mantra of most teachers—more time to prepare lessons, more time to collaborate. "If we had more time we could be so much more effective." But, the problem may not be that we don't have enough time; we simply may not be using the time we have in the best way for the results we seek.

Another common problem is that some teachers are pack rats. They like to hold on to the lessons that have served them well throughout the years. Just because something is your favorite lesson and the kids really like it, doesn't mean students are learning what they need from it. The educational world today is not the same world it was 10 or 20 years ago. Many of us realize this and are open to learning new things, but at the same time we have great difficulty throwing out the old "stuff." So we keep adding things to our repertoire without deleting anything. Imagine if you did that with your computer! After a while, it would run so slowly it would become ineffective. That's why we suggest that as you add new strategies and techniques, you think of old ones you can delete . That may be scary, but in the end it will make you a more effective teacher. At the same time, we're going to explore different ways to use your time to build critical thinking skills, while maximizing the learning experience for your students. It will mean changing how much time you spend intentionally teaching critical thinking skills, which is really the final goal.

What About Review Time?

One easy way to create more time in the classroom is to cut back on the amount of review time. The TIMMS study of 1999 found that 50% of what we instruct as teachers is actually review. One of the reasons we do this is because we don't always know exactly where our students can begin. If we counted more on the concept of formative assessment, specifically pretests, we'd have a better idea. Some would argue we're already testing kids to death; one more and there will not be any time left to actually teach them. But imagine being able to cut out a day's or even a week's worth of review for every unit you teach—that could literally transfer to weeks of new instructional time.

In addition, when you ask students to think at a higher level, you're essentially creating a situation where they have to review the content. For example, if you ask students to analyze how an author's choice of genre affects the expression of a theme, the students have to first review in their minds exactly what the theme is.

We suggest that teachers take a hard look at how they currently use their time. To help you do this, a pie chart titled *Instructional Time Distribution Graph* is provided in the Blueprints section. This activity will help you better understand how you're using your time, and if you need to redistribute it to accommodate the teaching of critical thinking skills.

How to Provide Time to Teach Critical Thinking

One way to redistribute your time is to intentionally ask higher-level thinking questions from the very beginning of a new unit. Deliberately resist the urge to review, and instead start students off with critical thinking questions to see if they respond. A good way to know if you even need to review is to give your students a pretest on the new content. Once you know what your students need, present it to them in a way in which they not only have to learn the material but actually extend their thinking. This comes from practice on your part.

For example, say you administer a pretest to your students in which you ask them to tell you the mood of a reading selection, and find that in this context, they don't know what the term "mood" means. The natural tendency is to provide the definition of mood to the students, giving them several reading selections where they have to identify what the mood of each selection is. To better employ higher-level thinking, consider instead providing the definition of mood, then asking students to explain or show what needs to happen to a selection to change the mood. Or, have them compare the moods of two different selections and tell how they're alike and different. You could even have the students predict what the mood would be if the setting were changed. Each of these examples requires students to do more to the concept of mood than just identify it—and in essence, they're demonstrating that they truly understand the meaning of the term "mood" and its implications to the plot of a story.

Another way to fix the review problem is to provide review only to those students who need it. You'll need to do some type of a pre-assessment to determine which students need review. A pre-assessment does not have to be pencil-to-paper; it can be as informal as a discussion where you use the term and see how students react. Once you've determined who has it and who doesn't, you'll need to differentiate your lesson groups. You can do that simply by providing work for two groups—one for review and one for new content. Try to use critical thinking activities in both. For example, let's say you're a 3rd grade teacher and one of the standards in social studies is:

> Identify the location of the equator, Arctic Circle, Antarctic Circle, North Pole, South Pole, Prime Meridian, the tropics, and the hemispheres on maps and globes.

You've determined through a pretest that about half your class has not yet mastered the skill of identifying the seven continents on a map—a prerequisite standard. You need to address the review issue, while at the same time moving those students who already understand the location of the seven continents forward. A simple way to do this is to provide two different learning activities. The review activity could be as simple as providing those students with a blank world map and a book that clearly labels the continents, and having them label their maps—not exactly higher-level thinking. What would create the need to think at a critical level, however, is to provide a Similarities and Differences Chart, and have the students list how the seven continents are the same and different. A completed chart such as this might look something like:

The Seven Continents

How They are the Same	How They are Different
• They all touch water. • North America, South America, Africa, Europe, and Asia all connect to other continents. • 5 of the continents are really big. • South America and Africa have about the same shape.	• Australia and Antarctica touch water on all sides while the others do not. • Australia and Antarctica do not touch any other continents. • Europe and Australia are not as big as the others. • Africa is divided up into a lot of small pieces while Australia is all one piece.

We've provided a blank *Similarities and Differences Chart* in the Blueprints section for your own use.

If you think that's too abstract for students, you could narrow the focus by providing an Analysis Sheet. That sheet might look like this:

List three ways Antarctica is the same as Australia:
1. They are both islands.
2. Their names both begin with the letter "A."
3. They are both at the bottom of the map.

List three ways Antarctica and Australia are different:
1. Antarctica is bigger than Australia.
2. Australia is closer to the other continents.
3. Antarctica is white on the map while Australia is green.

What you have when students have completed this activity is a springboard for all kinds of questions. These questions might include:

- What do you think those small "pieces" are in Africa? Why doesn't Australia have those?

- Why do you think Antarctica is colored white on this map?

- Why are there separate continents? Why aren't Europe and Asia one big continent?

- If you could live on any continent, where would it be and why?

- Would you rather live in Australia or Antarctica? Why?

These questions could be part of an oral discussion or could serve as writing prompts. The important thing is that rather than just giving students a map to label, you're intentionally requiring them to think at a higher level. This will lead students to put meaning into the activity, and subsequently they will be more likely to remember the continents in the future for enduring understanding—not to mention the fact you've raised the rigor in the classroom.

For those students who do not need basic review of the seven continents, you could simply provide a blank map and ask them to label the continents. Then move on to the standard to identify the Equator, the Arctic Circle, the Antarctic Circle, etc., by providing a map showing the location of these and instructing students to add them to their maps. To take it to a higher level, those students could work in groups to come up with specifics of each of these locations and a way to teach them to the other group, perhaps by providing a color-coded map, some type of mnemonic such as a song or a rhyme that would help them remember, or even by creating a world map puzzle.

By handling review in this manner, students at every level are being asked to think at a higher level rather than simply to label and define. This critical thinking element is what will add rigor to the curriculum—and while we understand the standard itself is being presented at a lower level (knowledge), by providing rigor to your students, everyone wins.

Specific Strategies to Teach Each of the Critical Levels of Bloom's

In previous chapters you were given ideas and suggestions about how to get students to think at the higher levels of Bloom's Taxonomy—*analysis, synthesis,* and *evaluation*. It's really about you being creative with your questioning—and the more you practice that skill, the easier it will become. Because that's a little abstract, this section will provide you with specific strategies for each of the levels.

To teach students how to analyze, you need to teach them to break apart information and examine those parts. With young children this can be done as a whole group, in several sittings, while with older students it can be done independently or in cooperative groups. To do that you guide them through the following steps:

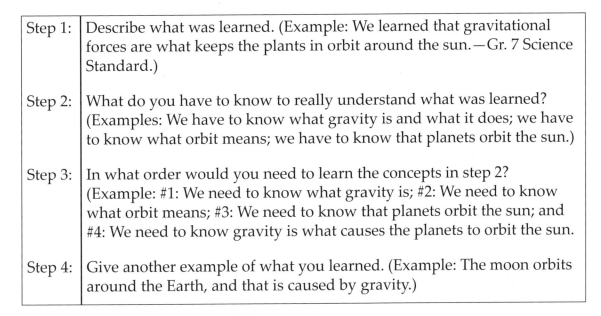

Step 1:	Describe what was learned. (Example: We learned that gravitational forces are what keeps the plants in orbit around the sun.—Gr. 7 Science Standard.)
Step 2:	What do you have to know to really understand what was learned? (Examples: We have to know what gravity is and what it does; we have to know what orbit means; we have to know that planets orbit the sun.)
Step 3:	In what order would you need to learn the concepts in step 2? (Example: #1: We need to know what gravity is; #2: We need to know what orbit means; #3: We need to know that planets orbit the sun; and #4: We need to know gravity is what causes the planets to orbit the sun.
Step 4:	Give another example of what you learned. (Example: The moon orbits around the Earth, and that is caused by gravity.)

A blank *Analysis Chart* is provided for you in the Blueprints section.

To teach students to synthesize, you need to teach them to put things they've learned together in a different way. They can make something completely new and different with the information or propose a completely different solution to a problem. The following steps will help you guide students through the synthesis level of thinking:

Step 1:	Describe what was learned. (Example: We learned how to add numbers. Gr. 1 Math Standard)
Step 2:	How did you learn it? (Example: We took four chips and put them on the table, then added more three more chips and counted them all up.)
Step 3:	What is a different way to do the same thing? (Example: We could draw pictures of the chips then count them up.)
Step 4:	What would happen if _____? (Example: What would happen if you had to take something away? What would you do?)

A blank *Synthesis Chart* is provided in the Blueprints section.

To teach students to evaluate, you need to teach them how to form an opinion and then how to defend it. You can teach them to look at the criteria first (how they are being asked to evaluate or judge) and then to make the judgment accordingly and list reasons to support their opinions. The following steps will help you guide your students through the evaluation level of thinking:

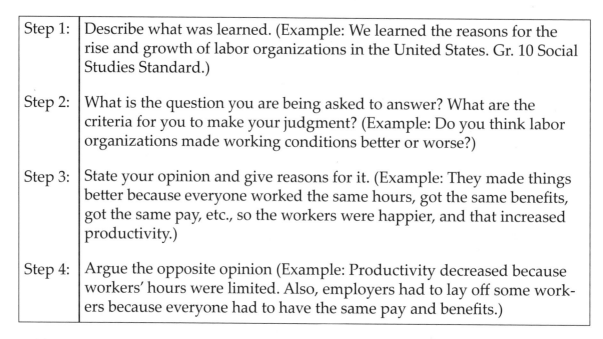

Step 1:	Describe what was learned. (Example: We learned the reasons for the rise and growth of labor organizations in the United States. Gr. 10 Social Studies Standard.)
Step 2:	What is the question you are being asked to answer? What are the criteria for you to make your judgment? (Example: Do you think labor organizations made working conditions better or worse?)
Step 3:	State your opinion and give reasons for it. (Example: They made things better because everyone worked the same hours, got the same benefits, got the same pay, etc., so the workers were happier, and that increased productivity.)
Step 4:	Argue the opposite opinion (Example: Productivity decreased because workers' hours were limited. Also, employers had to lay off some workers because everyone had to have the same pay and benefits.)

A blank *Evaluation Chart* is provided in the Blueprints section of this book.

The "Critical" Part of Instructional Strategies to Develop Critical Thinking Skills in the Classroom

Teaching critical thinking skills to all students—no matter the age, grade level, or subject matter—involves planning and practice on the part of the teacher. This may require you to "clean up your desktop" by eliminating certain things from your repertoire as you integrate rigor into your curriculum. Doing this may mean changing the amount of time you spend on review activities by pre-assessing for previously learned information and then differentiating instruction accordingly.

There are specific steps you can follow to ignite the type of critical thinking you want your students to use. The easy-to-follow steps are laid out for you both in narrative form in this chapter, and in chart form in the Blueprints section. Employing these strategies, as well as some of the other suggestions provided throughout the book will dramatically increase the amount of time your students spend thinking at a higher level in your classroom. Keep in mind that in the beginning you'll need to model for your students to demonstrate how to think at a higher level. We suggest you show them how you'd work through the different levels.

Also, don't be afraid to use the terms "analyze," "synthesize," and "evaluate" as well as "higher-level thinking," "critical thinking," and "rigor" in your day-to-day classroom vernacular. Even at a young age, students can learn to differentiate between the levels of thinking to identify lower and higher levels. Using higher-level thinking in your classroom every day will strengthen both your ability to teach higher-level thinking skills and your students' ability to think critically. By raising the rigor in your classroom, you will increase achievement, motivation, and interest for all students.

Epilogue:
Where to Go From Here

Do not go where the path may lead; go instead where there is no path and leave a trail.

Ralph Waldo Emerson

Leading the charge into the world of critical thinking will involve a lot of commitment and perseverance. The most important thing to remember is to start small. One way to do this is by simply integrating higher level thinking questions into your daily oral questioning and discussion time. Instead of being satisfied with a student response, try to ask one more question. Become skilled in the process of asking questions—let one question lead to another, which leads to another, and so on (i.e., the Socratic Method).

Another important thing to do when teaching students critical thinking skills is to constantly model that type of thinking for them. When your students ask you a question, go through your own thought processes out loud as you form your answer. Continually look for graphic organizers to make the process of idea organization easier. Have the students become proficient at identifying which questions are higher and lower level, and why.

As you integrate critical thinking questions into your formative assessments and instruction, remember you need to let some things go. Think of it as spring cleaning. Specifically, throw out those things that are not getting you the results you want no matter how fun and popular they are. As you look at the data connected to your formative assessments, explore ways to improve your teaching in response to the data. Read a book on differentiated instruction, or attend a conference on critical thinking strategies. Start a professional learning community within your school or work within your already formed PLC and share the challenges of teaching critical thinking skills. After all, two heads are better than one.

Finally, challenge yourself to add rigor to your classroom. Think of your students as your own children when you think of your expectations. Continue to read research that supports adding rigor to your classroom—particularly in the area of increased student achievement. Know by adding rigor to your classroom and teaching your students critical thinking skills, you are indeed doing what is best for students ... and the bottom line is, that is what it is really all about.

Part II

Blueprints
for the Process

This section is designed to give you the blueprints needed to integrate critical thinking and rigor into your formative assessments as well as your instructional practices. Here you will find activities, blank forms, handouts, and anything else needed for you to follow the steps that have been laid out for you in the chapters you have just read.

1. The Old Bloom's and the New Bloom's: What's the Diff??
2. What Level of Thinking Is It?
3. Higher-Level Questions for Younger Learners
4. How To Write Multiple Choice Questions for All Levels of Thinking
5. At What Level Am I Asking My Students To Think?
6. How To Write a Two-Part Multiple Choice Question
7. I Can ....
8. How I Would Instruct It/How I Would Assess It
9. Questions Conversion Chart
10. The Taxonomy Table
11. A Completed Taxonomy Table
12. Curriculum Pacing Guide
13. Leveled Pacing Guide
14. Sample Questions
15. Short-Cycle Assessment Checklist
16. Critical Thinking Flowchart
17. Developing Answer Rubrics for Critical Thinking Questions
18. Detailed Answer Key
19. Critical Thinking Data Chart
20. Class Profile Graph for Critical Thinking Questions
21. Proficiency on Critical Thinking Items Chart
22. Critical Thinking Item Analysis Graph
23. Questions To Ask When Analyzing Data with Regard to Critical Thinking Skills
24. Instructional Time Distribution Graph
25. Similarities and Differences Chart
26. Analysis Chart
27. Synthesis Chart
28. Evaluation Chart

1. The Old Bloom's and the New Bloom's: What's the Diff??

Original Bloom's Taxonomy	Revised Bloom's Taxonomy
Level I: Knowledge The student will exhibit memory of previously learned material by recall.	**Level I: Remembering** I can retrieve information already learned by recognizing or recalling.
Level II: Comprehension The student will demonstrate comprehension of facts or concepts.	**Level II: Understanding** I can show that I understand information that I have previously learned.
Level III: Application The student will solve problems for new situations by applying knowledge previously learned.	**Level III: Applying** I can use something that I have previously learned in a new way.
Level IV: Analysis The student will examine and break apart information to find relationships.	**Level IV: Analyzing** I can break down information into parts and show how the parts relate to one another.
Level V: Synthesis The student will compile information in a different way through a new pattern or different solution.	**Level V: Evaluating** I can form an opinion or make a judgment based on criteria and standards.
Level VI: Evaluation The student will present and defend opinions or make judgments according to a set of criteria.	**Level VI: Creating** I can put together elements I have learned to form a new product.

2. What Level of Thinking Is It?

Read each question and decide at what level you think the question is being asked. Use the letters below to code your answers. Then, write a one- or two-word justification for your answer. The answers can be found at the end of the activity.

Key	
K = Knowledge	An = Analysis
C = Comprehension	S = Synthesis
Ap = Application	E = Evaluation

The correct answer is marked with *.

1. What is the name of the rule in baseball when a fly ball is popped up into the infield and there are less than two outs with runners on first and second base?

   A. The Two-Out Fly Rule
   * B. The Infield Fly Rule
   C. The Infield Two-Out Rule
   D. The Infield Out Rule

   Level of Question = _____

   Justification: _____

   _____

   _____

2. Explain what the infield fly rule in baseball means. Why was this rule made?

   The infield fly rule takes effect when there are less than two outs in baseball and a ball is popped up into the infield with runners on two or more consecutive bases. In this case the batter is automatically out whether or not the infielder catches the ball. This rule was made to prevent infielders from intentionally missing the fly ball and then being able to throw the base runners out resulting in a double play.

   Level of Question = _____

   Justification: _____

   _____

   _____

3. Of the following statements, which best characterizes the difference between Calcium and Chlorine?

    A. There is a difference of 28 protons.

* B. Calcium is an alkaline earth metal while Chlorine is a nonmetal.

    C. The size of atoms in Calcium is much larger than in Chlorine.

    D. Calcium has a different number of electrons on the outside of its atoms than Chlorine does.

Level of Question = _____

Justification: _____

_____

_____

4. Which book do you think has a friendlier main character, *Goldilocks and the Three Bears* or *Little Red Riding Hood*? Support your answer using the text of the story you choose.

> * *I think that* Little Red Riding Hood *has the friendlier main character because the story says that Little Red Riding Hood is going to visit her grandmother and that is a very kind thing to do.*

Level of Question = _____

Justification: _____

_____

_____

5. Work the following problem:

$$3459$$
$$x \quad 75$$

    * *259,425*

Level of Question = _____

Justification: _____

_____

_____

6. Do you agree with what Goldilocks did when she came upon the house in the woods? Explain why or why not.

   No, I do not agree with what Goldilocks did when she came upon the house in the woods. It was wrong for her to go into the Three Bears' house because the house did not belong to her.

Level of Question = _____

Justification: _____

_____

_____

7. When John surveyed 50 students at his high school concerning school lunches he found that 25 students brought lunches from home. John predicted that half of the students in his state would not eat the school lunches. What is misleading about John's prediction? What is a valid prediction that John could have made from his survey results?

   John's prediction is misleading because he is assuming that half of the state's students bring their lunches from home. Also, he is assuming that all the students who buy school lunches will eat them. A valid prediction that John could make from his survey results would be that half of the students in his school bought school lunches each day.

Level of Question = _____

Justification: _____

_____

_____

8. From the selection, identify what *laissez-faire* economics means with regard to government.

   * A. Little government involvement
     B. Much government involvement
     C. Economics using small businesses
     D. Economics using large businesses

Level of Question = _____

Justification: _____

_____

_____

9. What is the setting of the book, *To Kill a Mockingbird*?

     A. A big city in the west
   * B. A small town in the south
     C. A ranch in the southwest
     D. A fishing village in the northwest

   Level of Question = _____

   Justification: _____

   _____

   _____

10. If the setting of the book, *To Kill a Mockingbird*, had been in the north instead of in the south, how might that have changed the story? Explain your answer.

     If the setting had been in the north instead of in the south, the perceptions of the African American characters in the book would have changed. The culture of the north was not as biased against African Americans as it was in the south, so the whole tone of the trial would have been less hostile.

   Level of Question = _____

   Justification: _____

   _____

   _____

What Level of Thinking Is It?

Answer Key:

1. Level: Knowledge
   Justification: The learner is recalling previously learned facts.

2. Level: Comprehension
   Justification: The learner is showing that s/he understands the rule.

3. Level: Analysis
   Justification: The learner is breaking down the two elements and finding differences between the two.

4. Level: Evaluation
   Justification: The learner is making a judgment based on a set of criteria.

5. Level: Application
   Justification: The learner is solving problems to a new situation by applying something s/he has already learned.

6. Level: Evaluation
   Justification: The learner is making a judgment based on a set of criteria.

7. Level: Synthesis
   Justification: The learner is compiling information in a different way to propose a different solution.

8. Level: Comprehension
   Justification: The learner is demonstrating that s/he understands what the term *laissez-faire* means

9. Level: Knowledge
   Justification: The learner is recalling previously learned facts.

10. Level: Analysis
    Justification The learner is having to examine and break apart information by looking at motives and causes.

3. Higher Level Questions for Younger Learners

The following are higher-level critical thinking questions that can be used with younger learners. We use these questions with common fairy tales, but feel free to adapt them to any story.

Story: *Goldilocks and the Three Bears* **Question:** Tell me what might have happened if Goldilocks had not run away at the end of the story.
Story: *Goldilocks and the Three Bears* **Question:** Which character do you like better in the story—Goldilocks or Baby Bear? Why do you feel this way?
Story: *Goldilocks and the Three Bears* **Question:** Do you think Goldilocks would have slept in the bed if she had burnt her mouth on the porridge? Tell why or why not.
Stories: *Goldilocks and the Three Bears* and *Little Red Riding Hood* **Question:** Tell me something that was the same about Goldilocks and Little Red Riding Hood as they were walking through the forest. Tell me something different about each character.
Story: *Little Red Riding Hood* **Question:** If Little Red Riding Hood had not stopped to pick the wildflowers as the Big Bad Wolf had suggested, how might that have changed the story?
Story: *Little Red Riding Hood* **Question:** If you were Little Red Riding Hood, would you have gone closer to the Big Bad Wolf when he was in the bed pretending to be Grandma? Why or why not?
Story: *Little Red Riding Hood* **Question:** Suppose the ending of the story remained the same. Change one thing that happened in the middle of the story that would have changed the story, but kept the ending the same.

Stories: *Little Red Riding Hood* and *Goldilocks and the Three Bears*   **Question:** If Little Red Riding Hood had met the Three Bears in the forest instead of the Big Bad Wolf, how might that have changed the story?
Story: *Jack and the Beanstalk*   **Question:** Would you have traded the cow for the beans if you were Jack? Why or why not?
Story: *Jack and the Beanstalk*   **Question:** How would the story have been different if Jack had not climbed the beanstalk?
Story: *Jack and the Beanstalk*   **Question:** Do you think Jack should have climbed up the beanstalk after he had the golden coins? Why or why not?
Story: *Jack and the Beanstalk*   **Question:** Why do you think the ogre's wife fed Jack? Would you have done the same thing? Why or why not?
Story: *Jack and the Beanstalk*   **Question:** Suppose Jack had not been able to cut down the beanstalk at the end of the story. Tell how the story might have ended.
Stories: *Jack and the Beanstalk* and *Goldilocks and the Three Bears*   **Question:** How are Jack and Goldilocks alike? How are they different?
Story: *Cinderella*   **Question:** Pretend that you are going to interview Cinderella. What is one question that you would ask her? Explain why you would ask this.
Story: *Cinderella*   **Question:** If you were Cinderella, how would you treat your step-mother and step-sisters after you become a princess? Explain.
Story: *Cinderella*   **Question:** Would you rather be Cinderella or the Fairy Godmother? Explain.

Story: Cinderella **Question:** What do you think happened to the magic slippers?
Story: Cinderella **Question:** If you were Cinderella, would you have left the ball at midnight? Explain why or why not.
Story: General **Question:** Could this story happen today? How would it be the same? How would it be different?
Story: General **Question:** What is the lesson being taught in the story?
Story: General **Question:** Make up a different ending for the story.
Story: General **Question:** Which character in the story do you like best and why?
Story: General **Question:** Do you agree with what (the main character) did? Why or why not? What would you do differently?

4. How To Write Multiple Choice Questions for All Levels of Thinking

Writing a multiple choice question is easy, once you know the formula. Just follow these three easy steps.

1. Think of the question you want to ask. Write the question. Make sure it assesses the standard.

   _____

   _____

   _____

2. Think of an answer that could be considered correct. Write that answer below in one of the choices A, B, C, or D.

   _____

   _____

   _____

3. Now, write the three distracters. The distracters need to sound plausible, yet be incorrect. Remember, no "goofy" or "far out" distracters. The distracters need to be similar in length.

   A. _____

   _____

   B. _____

   _____

   C. _____

   _____

   D. _____

   _____

Now, put them all together and you have a multiple choice question. Remember to vary the letter under which you put the correct answer.

5. At What Level Am I Asking My Students To Think?

When trying to decide at which level of Bloom's Taxonomy a certain question or activity is, it is sometimes helpful to look at the type of thinking required of the students rather than just the key words and question stems. Use this blueprint when you are having a difficult time ascertaining the level of a question or activity.

Write the question or describe the activity here:

_____

_____

Now, ask yourself

"Am I asking my students to exhibit memory of previously-learned material by recalling facts, terms, basic concepts, and answers?"

If the answer is "Yes," then the question is at a **knowledge** level.

If you think the students are being asked to do more than that, ask yourself,

"Am I asking my students to demonstrate understanding by organizing, comparing, translating, interpreting, giving descriptions, and stating main ideas?"

If the answer is "Yes," then the question is at a **comprehension** level.

If you think the students are being asked to do more than that, ask yourself,

"Am I asking my students to solve problems for new situations by applying learned knowledge, facts, or rules in a different way?"

If the answer is "Yes," then the question is at an **application** level.

If you think the students are being asked to do more than that, ask yourself,

"Am I asking my students to examine and break information into parts by looking at motives, causes, and relationships?"

If the answer is "Yes," then the question is at an **analysis** level.

If you think the students are being asked to do more than that, ask yourself,

> "Am I asking my students to put information together in a different way by combining elements in a new pattern or proposing a different solution?"
>
> If the answer is "Yes," then the question is at a **synthesis** level.

If you think the students are being asked to do more than that, ask yourself,

> "Am I asking my students to present and defend an opinion or make a judgment based on a set of criteria?
>
> If the answer is "Yes," then the question is at an **evaluation** level.

If after all of this you still don't know, consider rewriting the question or changing the activity so that it meets the level you are trying to achieve.

6. How To Write a Two-Part Multiple Choice Question

There are some simple rules that apply to all multiple choice questions, whether they are lower-level or higher-level questions. These rules are:

- The question may have one part or more than one part.

- The distracters (answer choices) should be similar; if one answer is a complete sentence, then all answers should be complete sentences; if one answer is a one-word answer, then all answers should be one-word answers, etc.

- There should be no "goofy," off-the-wall answers. All of the choices should be logical, plausible answers.

- It is sometimes a good idea to include the words "Choose the best answer" in your question if there is more than one answer that could be correct.

The following template will help you to write a two-part multiple choice question at any level. Try writing one now. An example of such a question using the story *Goldilocks and the Three Bears* is: Which bear cried when he discovered that Goldilocks had sat in his chair? Why do you think he reacted that way?

Now, write your question below specifying the two parts:

Question Part I: _____

_____

Question Part II: _____

_____

Next, you will need to provide the correct answer for your question. If your question is a lower-level question, it will only have one correct answer. If your question is a higher-level question, there may be several possible correct answers. In this case, choose an answer that you would be willing to accept as correct. For example, the Goldilocks question could have a couple of correct answers. One might be,

"Baby Bear because he was sad that his chair was broken."

Another correct answer might be,

"Baby Bear because the broken chair was his favorite chair."

Try to choose the correct answer that is the clearest and most plausible answer.

Now, write the correct answer to the question you wrote:

Correct Answer: _____

_____

_____

Next, write the distracters. Remember, they need to look similar to the answer. It is easy to write distracters for a two-part question if you use the following formula:

Answer Choice #1: part #1 correct, part #2 correct
Answer Choice #2: part #1 correct, part #2 incorrect
Answer Choice #3: part #1 incorrect, part #2 correct
Answer Choice #4: part #1 incorrect, part #2 incorrect

Using this formula, the answers for the Goldilocks question would look like this:

A. Baby Bear because the broken chair was his favorite chair.
B. Baby Bear because the broken chair was his father's chair.
C. Mama Bear, because the broken chair was her favorite chair.
D. Mama Bear, because the broken chair was Papa Bear's chair.

Now, write your three distracters using the formula for Answer Choices # 2, 3, and 4.

Answer Choice # 2: _____

_____

Answer Choice # 3: _____

_____

Answer Choice # 4: _____

_____

The last step is to put the question and all four answer choices together. Remember to vary where you place the correct answer—don't use C each time!!!

Question:

A.
B.
C.
D.

7. I Can ....

Take each of the academic content standards for your subject area and rewrite them as an "I Can ..." statement. Most times, this can be done by simply adding the words "I can" to the beginning of the standard. For example, the standard,

> "Extend multiplicative and growing patterns, and describe the pattern or rule in words."

becomes: As a third-grade math student, "I can extend multiplicative and growing patterns, and I can describe the pattern or rule in words."

Standard	"I Can" Statement

8. How I Would Instruct It/How I Would Assess It

List each of your academic content standards in the middle of the chart. Then, describe how you would instruct that standard in the column on the left side. Next, decide how you will assess that standard and write this information on the right side. Be as specific as you can.

Teacher's Name _____ Grade _____ Subject Area _____

How I Would Instruct It	Academic Content Standard	How I Would Assess It

93 © Eye On Education • Critical Thinking and Formative Assessments • Moore and Stanley

9. Questions Conversion Chart

You can use the released tests found on your state's Department of Education website to determine the number and types of questions on your state assessment. It is recommended that you use two of the tests for your subject area to make sure the average is consistent, but it is not mandatory.

Total number of questions
on the state assessment   _____ carry # down through this column

Number of multiple choice
questions   (____ pts.)   _____ ÷ _____ X   20 = _____ questions

Number of constructed response
questions   (____ pts.)   _____ ÷ _____ X   20 = _____ questions

Number of constructed response
questions   (____ pts.)   _____ ÷ _____ X   20 = _____ questions

Number of constructed response
questions   (____ pts.)   _____ ÷ _____ X   20 = _____ questions

Number of response grid
questions   _____ ÷ _____ X   20 = _____ questions

Number of written
responses   _____ ÷ _____ X   20 = _____ questions

10. The Taxonomy Table

Analyze the content standards looking at the verb and determining the level of the grade-level indicator.

Subject/Grade:

Description of Standard	Knowledge	Comprehension	Application	Analysis	Synthesis	Evaluation

11. A Completed Taxonomy Table

Analyze the content standards looking at the verb and determining the level of the grade-level indicator.

Subject/Grade: Math/Grade 8 Description of Standard	Knowledge	Comprehension	Application	Analysis	Synthesis	Evaluation
Number, Number Sense, and Operations		#1	#2			#3
Measurement			#4	#5		
Geometry				#4	#7	
Patterns, Functions, and Algebra	#8	#9				#10
Data Analysis and Probability	#11					#12

Standard Descriptors for a Completed Taxonomy Table

Standard Descriptors

Number, Number Sense, and Operations

1. Recognize that natural numbers, whole numbers, integers, rational numbers, and irrational numbers are subsets of the real number system.
2. Explain and use the inverse and identity properties and use inverse relationships in problem-solving situations.
3. Determine when an estimate is sufficient and when an exact answer is needed in problem-solving situations.

Measurement

4. Use appropriate levels of precision when calculating with measurements.
5. Compare and order the relative size of common U.S. customary units and metric units.

Geometry

6. Represent and analyze shapes using coordinate geometry.
7. Make and test conjectures about characteristics and properties of two-dimensional figures and three-dimensional objects.

Patterns, Functions, and Algebra

8. Identify functions as linear or nonlinear based on information given in a table, graph, or equation.
9. Generalize patterns and sequences by describing how to find the nth term.
10. Write, simplify, and evaluate algebraic expressions to generalize situations and solve problems.

Data Analysis and Probability

11. Identify different ways of selecting samples, such as survey response, random sample, representative sample, and convenience sample.
12. Construct convincing arguments based on analysis of data and interpretation of graphs.

12. Curriculum Pacing Guide

School District _____ Grade Level _____ Subject Area _____

Grading Period 1 *Standards*	Grading Period 2 *Standards*	Grading Period 3 *Standards*	Grading Period 4 *Standards*

13. Leveled Pacing Guide

School/District _____   Grade Level _____   Subject Area _____

Level	Grading Period 1	Grading Period 2	Grading Period 3	Grading Period 4
Knowledge				
Comprehension				
Application				
Analysis				
Synthesis				
Evaluation				

14. Sample Questions

The following questions are meant to be used to help you deepen your understanding of questions written at the different levels. You may use these questions as they are, "tweak" them to fit your circumstances, or use them as a template for new questions.

Reading Knowledge-Level Sample Questions

- Place a book in front of a child. Ask him or her to do the following: Find the front of the book. Look at all of the pictures. Go to the first page. Show me where you start reading. Where do you go from here? After the first line, ask: Where do you go next? Point to the illustrations. Point to the print.

  Put a checkmark next to the tasks the child can do.

  ___ finds front of book
  ___ reads from front to back
  ___ left to right
  ___ return sweep
  ___ identifies illustrations
  ___ identifies print

  Answer Rubric:
  1 point for each skill.

  Assessing Alabama Standard for Grade 1: Identify parts of a book.

- In the first stanza of the poem the poet uses the image of a woman sighing, laughing, and humming to represent the sounds of the wind blowing in different places. This is an example of

  A. rhyme
  B. personification
  C. rhythm

  Assessing Pennsylvania Standard for Grade 3: Identify literary devices in stories (e.g., rhyme, rhythm, personification).

Reading Comprehension-Level Sample Questions

- Read the following statement.

    "Children should be allowed to pick out their own books in the library."

    What makes this an opinion and not a fact? Choose the best answer.

    A. It is an opinion because it is not backed up with proof.
    B. It is an opinion because it voices what the writer feels.
    C. It is an opinion because it is backed up with data.
    D. It is an opinion because everyone knows it is what is best.

    Assessing Texas Standard for Grade 5: Distinguish fact from opinion.

- What is the setting in the book *Bridge to Terabithia*? Describe the setting using at least 3 details.

    Answer Rubric:
    1 point for telling the answer to the question: The setting is in a forest.
    1 point for providing a description of the setting using at least three details.

    Assessing Kansas Standard for Grade 4: Identify and describe the setting (e.g., environment, time of day or year, historical period, situation, place) of the story or literary text.

Reading Application-Level Sample Questions

- Which of the following books would you use if you wanted to be informed—
  All About Giraffes or *Gerald Giraffe's Birthday Party?*

Tell why you would choose that book.

> Answer Rubric:
> 1 point for choosing the book *All About Giraffes.*
> 1 point for telling why: e.g.,"Because it will give me information about
> giraffes," or "It will tell me about giraffes while the other book is a story."

*Assessing North Dakota Standard for Grade 2: Use reading to be informed, persuaded,
and entertained. Students consistently make text choices that are appropriate to the
reading purpose.*

- Read the following paragraph from the article "Yellowstone Makes a
  Triumphant Return Ten Years After Fires" by Bruce Babbitt, Former Sec-
  retary of the Interior, originally printed in *The Austin American-Statesman.*

> What a difference a decade makes. Ten years ago this month, Yellowstone
> National Park was a sea of flames. Some of the largest wildfires in U.S. his-
> tory swept relentlessly across the park's magnificent terrain, incinerating
> forests, threatening historic buildings. The news media and politicians
> fanned the flames even higher. Yellowstone, they said, was devastated.
> Night after night, horrific images of ash and flame flashed across America's
> TV screens. One evening, after showing an enormous expanse of blackened
> forest, network news anchor Tom Brokaw solemnly concluded, "This is
> what's left of Yellowstone tonight."

Which of these subheadings would most accurately reflect the information in
this paragraph?

> A. Effects of the Yellowstone Fire
> B. Tourism Since the Yellowstone Fire
> **C. News Media Dramatically Reports Fire**
> D. Biodiversity in Yellowstone Since the Fire

*Assessing Alaska Standard for Grade 9: Restate and summarize main ideas or events,
in correct sequence, after reading a text (e.g., paraphrasing, constructing a topic outline, charting, or mapping main ideas or events) or identify accurate restatements and
summaries of main ideas or events or generalizations of a text.*

Reading Analysis-Level Sample Questions

- If the setting to *Bridge to Terabithia* had been in a city instead of a rural town, do you think that might have changed the problem of the story and its resolution, and why?

    Answer Rubric:
    1 point for telling how the setting might have changed the problem and resolution.
    1 point for telling why.

    Assessing Indiana Standard for Grade 6: Analyze the influence of the setting on the problem and its resolution.

- In the book, *The Biography of Helen Keller*, the conflict is Helen's inability to communicate. Fill in the Venn Diagram below by telling how the viewpoints of each of the main characters are alike and how they are different with regard to the conflict.

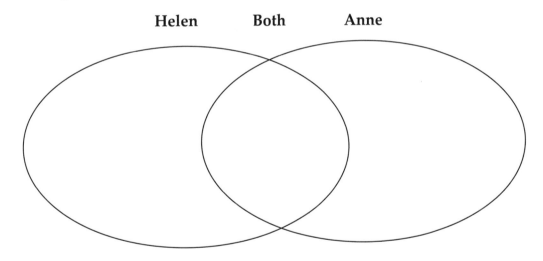

Helen   Both   Anne

    Answer Rubric:
    1 point for telling how the viewpoints of Helen and Anne were alike—Example: Both are frustrated when Helen cannot communicate.
    1 point for telling how Helen and Anne were different—Example: Helen thought Anne was mean and didn't like her while Anne liked Helen and wanted what was best for her.

    Assessing Connecticut Standard for Grade 5: Compare and contrast the same conflict from the point of view of two different characters.

Reading Synthesis-Level Sample Questions

- Use the map of the United States shown above and the graph of Population Density to answer the following question.

  Which topographical feature has the most influence on population density?

  A. mountain ranges
  B. water sources
  C. deserts
  D. swampland

  *Answers will depend on the map and graph provided to the students.

  Assessing Arizona Standard for Grade 10: Synthesize information from multiple sources (e.g., texts, maps, illustrations, workplace documents, schematic diagrams) to solve a problem.

- Describe two ways the plot of the book, *To Kill A Mockingbird* might be different if the story was set in the North instead of in the South. Give reasons for your answers.

  Answer Rubric:
    1 point for telling one way the plot might be different.
    1 point for giving a reason.
    1 point for telling another way the plot might be different.
    1 point for giving a reason.

  Assessing Illinois Standard for Grade 7: Predict how the story might be different if the author changed certain literary elements or techniques (e.g., dialect, setting, vocabulary).

Reading Evaluation-Level Sample Questions

- Which "just right" book would you choose if you needed to find out about elephants, and why would you choose this book?

  A. *Eddie the Elephant Takes a Nap* because it is a funny book.
  B. *Learning About Zoo Animals* because an elephant is a zoo animal.
  C. *Elephant and Pig Become Friends* because it is about getting along.

  Assessing Connecticut Standard for Grade 2: Select "just right" books of different genres for independent reading, and explain why the book choice was appropriate.

- Explain the purpose Malcolm X had in writing the passage above. Do you agree with his purpose? Use details from the selection to support your answer.

  Answer Rubric:
  1 point for explaining the purpose.
  1 point for stating "yes" or "no" and providing support.

  Assessing Minnesota Standard for Grade 7: Critically read and evaluate to determine the author's purpose.

Writing Knowledge-Level Sample Questions

• In which of the following sentences are the subject and verb in agreement?

   A. We is going to the store.
   B. They are having a party.
   C. She are getting a new bike.

   Assessing Indiana Standard for Grade 3: Identify subjects and verbs that are in agreement.

• Which of the following is an example of an analogy?

   A. The wind was blowing so hard you could feel the dust pierce your skin.
   B. The wind was blowing so hard you felt as if you were a scrap of paper caught in a fan.
   C. The wind was blowing so hard you couldn't see two feet in front of you.
   D. The wind was blowing so hard it blew your feet out from under you.

   Assessing Illinois Standard for Grade 8: Identify and use analogy in writing.

Writing Comprehension-Level Sample Questions

- Copy this sentence: I like the zoo because it is fun to see the animals.

  Now, write this sentence in your own words: I like the zoo because it is fun to see the animals.

  Answer Rubric:
  1 point for copying the sentence correctly.
  1 point for writing the sentence in your own words—Example: "The zoo is fun because the animals are fun to watch," etc.

  Assessing Kansas Standard for Grade 1: Understand the difference between copying and using one's own words.

- Lily is writing about how to make a three-layer cake. Which form of writing should she use?

  A. description
  B step-by-step instructions
  C observation
  D informative report

  Assessing Alaska Standard for Grade 6: Write in a variety of nonfiction forms using appropriate information and structure (i.e., step-by-step directions, descriptions, observations, or report writing).

Writing Application-Level Sample Questions

- Rewrite the following paragraph. Correct the errors in grammar and usage, as well as the errors in mechanics.

  This was Walter's second day at Meadowbrook elementary school. He were slowly learning his way around, but with so many hallways it were not easy. Walter took his pet mouse to school one day After completing a quiz, walter decided to go to the playground. Soon he realized he didn't know where to go? he walked to the end of the hall looked both ways, and turned around. As he started back down the hall, he saw his teacher. "Is everything okay, Walter"? she asked. "No, Mrs. Connors," replied Walter. "I cannot find the door to the playground." mrs Connors smiled and led Walter to the right door. Walter smiled and thanked she.

  Answer Rubric:
  1 point for correcting all of the grammar errors.
  1 point for correcting all of the mechanical errors.

  This was Walter's second day at Meadowbrook Elementary School. He was slowly learning his way around, but with so many hallways it was not easy. Walter took his pet mouse to school one day. After completing a quiz, Walter decided to go to the playground. Soon he realized he didn't know where to go. He walked to the end of the hall, looked both ways, and turned around. As he started back down the hall, he saw his teacher. "Is everything okay, Walter?" she asked. "No, Mrs. Connors," replied Walter. "I cannot find the door to the playground." Mrs. Connors smiled and led Walter to the right door. Walter smiled and thanked her.

  Assessing Alabama Standard for Grade 4: Know and apply principles of grammar and usage in writing, speaking, and presenting and apply mechanics in writing.

- Read the following sentence.

  "As the soldier lay dying, a gurgling rattle came from deep within him."

  Why would the author choose to use onomatopoeia to describe the dying soldier?

  A. The author is trying to paint a descriptive picture of the death process.
  B. The author is trying to show how disturbing war can be.
  C. The author is trying to prove that the soldier is indeed dying.
  D. The author is trying to keep the reader from knowing what is happening.

  Assessing North Dakota Standard for Grade 8: Explain the uses of sound devices in literary texts, including alliteration, onomatopoeia, rhyme, repetition, and rhythm.

Writing Analysis-Level Sample Questions

- Where should the following sentence below be inserted into the numbered paragraph?

This layer prevents air and water from damaging the metal.

1. Car makers have come up with ways to protect vehicles from rust.
2. Usually, they apply a coat of zinc to the iron used in cars. 3. As long as this coating is not damaged, the car will stay rust free.

- A. Before sentence 1

  This layer prevents air and water from damaging the metal. Car makers have come up with ways to protect vehicles from rust. Usually, they apply a coat of zinc to the iron used in cars. As long as this coating is not damaged, the car will stay rust free.

- B. Before sentence 2

  Car makers have come up with ways to protect vehicles from rust. *This layer prevents air and water from damaging the metal.* Usually, they apply a coat of zinc to the iron used in cars. As long as this coating is not damaged, the car will stay rust free.

- **C. Before sentence 3**

  Car makers have come up with ways to protect vehicles from rust. Usually, they apply a coat of zinc to the iron used in cars. *This layer prevents air and water from damaging the metal.* As long as this coating is not damaged, the car will stay rust free.

- D. After sentence 3

  Car makers have come up with ways to protect vehicles from rust. Usually, they apply a coat of zinc to the iron used in cars. As long as this coating is not damaged, the car will stay rust free. *This layer prevents air and water from damaging the metal.*

from the Ohio Achievement Test—Writing Grade 7, 2008

Assessing Ohio Standard for Grade 7: Reread and analyze clarity of writing.

- Read the two excepts about the life of Anne Frank. Describe the similarities and differences in the two pieces. Which piece do you think did a better job of portraying the tragedy of Anne Frank's life? Support your answer with details from the text.

  Answer Rubric:
  1 point for describing the similarities.
  1 point for describing the differences.
  1 point for stating which piece did a better job of portraying the tragedy of Anne Frank's life.
  1 point for supporting the answer with details from text.

  Assessing Arizona Standard for Grade 9: Compare works within a literary genre that deal with similar themes (e.g., compare two short stories or two poems).

Writing Synthesis-Level Sample Questions

- Read each of the arguments for and against the death penalty carefully, then come up with a compromise. Write about your compromise and support it using the information from both articles.

  Answer Rubric:
    2 points for writing a well-organized piece that contains the compromise and supports the position with at least one reference to each article.
    1 point for writing a piece that contains the compromise but does not reference both articles.
    0 points for writing a piece that does not contain either a compromise or reference to the articles.

  Assessing Connecticut Standard for Grade 8: Analyze and synthesize information from multiple resources to establish and support a position, and to examine opposing perspectives.

- Write a persuasive paragraph arguing for the need for more playground equipment at your school. Keep in mind that your audience will be the parents who will donate the time, money, and manpower to build the new playground equipment. Make sure that you include a topic sentence, body, and closing sentence in your paragraph.

  Answer Rubric:
    2 points for writing a well-organized persuasive paragraph that contains all the elements: topic sentence, body and closing sentence.
    1 point for writing a paragraph that is persuasive but lacks some of the elements for a paragraph: topic sentence, body or closing sentence.
    0 points for writing a paragraph that does not persuade the reader and/ or does not contain any of the elements for a paragraph: topic sentence, body, and closing sentence.

  Assessing Minnesota Standard for Grade 5: Consider the intended audience when composing text.

Writing Evaluation-Level Sample Questions

- Read the following paragraph.

  Springtime is a time of many weather activities. There are a lot of warm days. There are many different blooms of colorful flowers. It is a good time to be outside enjoying the sunshine. Yet, sometimes there are tornados with fierce winds. Easter is in the springtime.

  According to the guidelines below, what does the writer need to improve when revising this paragraph?

  Guidelines:
  1. The paper contains a clear purpose and a central theme.
  2. The word choice is clear and accurate.
  3. The sentences are varied and flow naturally.
  4. The paper is free of punctuation and capitalization errors.

     A. Guideline 1
     B. Guideline 2
     C. Guideline 3
     D. Guideline 4

Assessing Texas Standard for Grade 8: Apply criteria to evaluate writing.

- Read the following poem.

Count That Day Lost

If you sit down at set of sun
And count the acts that you have done,
And, counting, find
One self-denying deed, one word
That eased the heart of him who heard,
One glance most kind
That fell like sunshine where it went—
Then you may count that day well spent.

But if, through all the livelong day,
You've cheered no heart, by yea or nay—
If, through it all
You've nothing done that you can trace
That brought the sunshine to one face—
No act most small
That helped some soul and nothing cost—
Then count that day as worse than lost.

by George Eliot

What message do you think the poet is sending? Do you agree with her? Explain why or why not using examples from the poem and your own experiences.

Answer Rubric:
  1 point for stating the message the poet is sending.
  1 point for stating "yes" or "no" and explaining why you agree or not.

Assessing Ohio Standard for Grade 4: Write responses to novels, stories and poems that include a simple interpretation of a literary work and support judgments with specific references to the original text and to prior knowledge.

Math Knowledge-Level Sample Questions

- Which of the following are odd numbers?

  A. 2, 5, 8, 9
  B. 1, 4, 7, 10
  C. 2, 4, 6, 8
  D. 1, 5, 7, 9

  Assessing Kentucky Standard for Grade 4: Students will identify and provide examples of odd and even numbers.

- According to the clock, what time is it?

  A. 10:50
  B. 11:50
  C. 9:45
  D. 9:55

  Assessing North Carolina Standard for Grade 2: Tell time at five-minute intervals.

Math Comprehension-Level Sample Questions

- $y = x^2$

  Use the following formula to complete the table.

x	y
2	
	1
0	
	9

  Answer Rubric:

x	y
2	4
1	1
0	0
3	9

  Assessing Georgia Standard for Grade 8: Use tables to describe sequences recursively and with a formula in closed form.

- Which of the following is the longest line?

  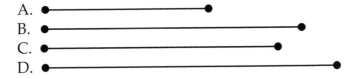

  A.
  B.
  C.
  D.

  Assessing Tennessee Standard for Kindergarten: Demonstrate understanding of the concept of length.

Math Application-Level Sample Questions

- What is the answer to the following problem?

    Answer Rubric: 20

Assessing Idaho Standard for Grade 2: Add three one-digit addends.

- Marcum's was having a sale on art supplies. The art easel was originally $100 and was then marked 50% off. Finally, the art easel went on clearance for 20% off of the sale price. How much could Mara get the art easel for?

    A. $30
    B. $40
    C. $50
    D. $40

Assessing Alaska Standard for Grade 10: Solving problems involving percent increase or decrease.

Math Analysis Level Sample Questions

- Which of the segments in the following circles is the larger of the two? Be sure to explain your answer.

a. 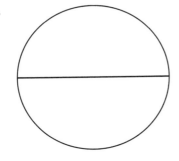 b.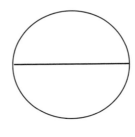

Answer Rubric:
  1 point for "a."
  1 point for explaining that half of "a" is larger because it is the larger of the circles, thus half of the larger circle will be larger than half of the smaller circle.

Assessing Illinois Standard for Grades 5 to 6: Analyze how the size of the whole affects the size of the fraction (e.g., 1/2 of a large pizza is not the same as 1/2 of a small pizza).

- Manning Lanes Bowling Scores

Thomas	152	196	145	167
Michael	142	145	142	147
Chris	117	88	140	108
Anthony	225	185	164	114

Which of the bowlers would be the best based on the mean?

A. Thomas
B. Michael
C. Chris
D. Anthony

Which of the bowlers is the most consistent based on the smallest range?

A. Thomas
B. Michael
C. Chris
D. Anthony

Comparing and contrasting the data, who would most likely score the highest if a fifth game was played?

A. Thomas
B. Michael
C. Chris
D. Anthony

Assessing Pennsylvania Standard for Grade 8: Compare and contrast different plots of data using values of mean, median, mode, quartiles, and range.

Math Synthesis-Level Sample Questions

- Heather had to solve the following problem:

$$3 \times 6 = \underline{\hspace{2cm}}$$

She solved it this way:

$$6 + 6 + 6 = 18.$$

Show a different way Heather could solve the problem to get the correct answer. Explain why your way works.

Answer Rubric:
  1 point for answering another way (e.g., $3 + 3 + 3 + 3 + 3 + 3 = 18$ or $3 \times 5 = 15$ and $15 + 3 = 18$).
  1 point for explaining the answer (e.g., Because $3 + 3 + 3 + 3 + 3 + 3$ is the number 3 added together 6 times and that is what 3×6 means, or because $3 \times 5 = 15$ and one more $3 = 18$).

Assessing Arizona Standard for Grade 3: Create and solve simple one-step equations that can be solved using addition and multiplication facts.

- Here is the forecast for the day:

Cloudy skies overnight. Low 47°F. Winds N at 10 to 15 mph. Chance of rain 80%.

What are the chances that the outdoor tennis match will occur?

A. definitely will not happen
B. will happen
C. likely
D. unlikely

Assessing South Carolina Standard for Grade 1: Predict on the basis of data whether events are likely or unlikely to occur.

Math Evaluation-Level Sample Questions

- Judge which of the following two solutions to the problem is better explained and explain why you chose this solution.

  Problem: Find the domain of $f(x) = \sqrt{3x} - 7$.

  Solution 1: $[7/3, \infty)$.
  Solution 2: Since $\sqrt{3x} - 7$ is defined only when the quantity under the radical is nonnegative, the domain is the solution to $3x - 7 \geq 0$. This requires $3x \geq 7$, which in turn requires $x \geq 7/3$. Therefore, the domain (in interval notation) is $[7/3, \infty)$.

  Answer Rubric:
    1 point for choosing Solution 2 as the best answer.
    1 point for explaining that because even though Solution 1 gets to the point, it doesn't say how it got there. It is better to show how you got the answer to prove you understand it.

  Assessing Texas Standard for Grade 7: Determine the reasonableness of a solution to a problem.

- The Perry County Commissioners hired an Activities Director for the summer. To plan her program, she surveyed the patients of all the nursing homes in the county. Does her survey represent the interests of all the residents of Perry County ? Explain your answer.

  Answer Rubric:
    1 point for no.
    1 point if answers include the fact that only one age group was used (and they are not very active!).

  Assessing Ohio Standard for Grade 10: Provide examples and explain how a statistic may or may not be an attribute of the entire population; e.g., intentional or unintentional bias may be present.

Social Studies Knowledge-Level Sample Questions

- What is separation of power? Name a political benefit for separation of power. What is a possible problem with separation of power? How could this problem be solved?

  Answer Rubric:
  1 point for separating government into three branches: legislative, executive, and judicial.
  1 point for explaining that it prevents any one branch from gaining too much power and abusing it.
  1 point for answers that include the separation of power slows down the political process and can cause things to take a while to happen, because different parties represent different branches and may cause conflict between them.
  1 point for answers that solve the problem brought up in the third answer (the separation of power slows down the political process and can cause things to take a while to happen); a solution would be to improve communication between the branches to make things go more quickly.

  Assessing Wisconsin Standard for Grade 12: Identify significant political benefits, problems, and solutions to problems related to federalism and the separation of powers.

- Complete the following:

January	May
February	June
_____	_____
April	August

  Answer Rubric:
January	May
February	June
<u>March</u>	<u>July</u>
April	August

  Assessing Ohio Standard for Grade 1: Recite the months of the year.

Social Studies Comprehension-Level Sample Questions

• The causes of the Great Depression are still a matter of active debate among economists. The specific economic events that took place during the Great Depression have been studied thoroughly: a deflation in asset and commodity prices, dramatic drops in demand and credit, and disruption of trade, ultimately resulting in widespread poverty and unemployment. However, historians lack consensus in describing the causal relationship among various events and the role of government economic policy in causing or ameliorating the Depression.

According to the passage, what was a cause of the Great Depression?
- A. unemployment
- B. the role of the government
- C. poverty
- **D. drops in demand and credit**

Assessing South Dakota Standard for Grade 10: Explain the factors that led to the Great Depression.

• Place the following events in order. Explain why you put them in the order you chose.

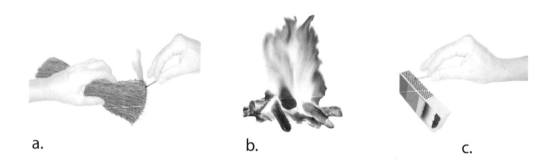

a.   b.   c.

Answer Rubric:
  1 point for the order c, a, b.
  1 point for explaining that one must light the match before flame can be created; the kindling must be lit in picture "a" before applying it to the bigger wood and stronger flame in picture "b."

Assessing Nebraska Standard for Kindergarten: Explain the past and the present through pictures, oral history, letters, or journals.

© Eye On Education • Critical Thinking and Formative Assessments • Moore and Stanley

Social Studies Application-Level Sample Questions

Map Of The Continental U.S.A.

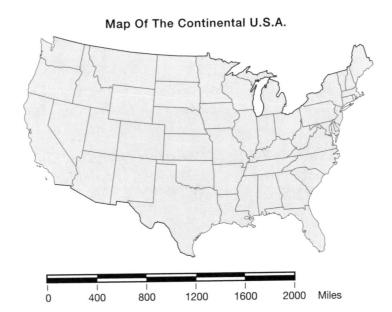

- Approximately how many miles is it across the United States?
  A. 1500
  B. 2000
  C. 2400
  D. 2700

  Assessing North Dakota Standard for Grade 4: Use map scales to locate physical features and estimate distance on a map.

- Construct a timeline where you put the following events in chronological order. Be sure to include the year they occurred.

  - Boston Tea Party
  - Battle at Lexington
  - Stamp Act
  - Declaration of Independence
  - Boston Massacre

  Answer Rubric:
      1 point for the correct order
      1 point for correct dates

| 1765 | 1770 | 1773 | 1775 | 1776 |
| Stamp Act | Boston Massacre | Boston Tea Party | Battle at Lexington | Declaration of Independence |

Assessing Oklahoma Standard for Grade 10: Construct timelines of United States history (e.g., landmark dates of economic changes, social movements, military conflicts, constitutional amendments, and presidential elections).

Social Studies Analysis-Level Sample Questions

...In my way there I saw the people in great commotion, and heard them use the most cruel and horrid threats against the troops. In a few minutes after I reached the guard, about 100 people passed it and went towards the custom house where the king's money is lodged. They immediately surrounded the sentry posted there, and with clubs and other weapons threatened to execute their vengeance on him. I was soon informed by a townsman their intention was to carry off the soldier from his post and probably murder him... I immediately sent a noncommissioned officer and 12 men to protect both the sentry and the king's money, and very soon followed myself to prevent, if possible, all disorder, fearing lest the officer and soldiers, by the insults and provocations of the rioters, should be thrown off their guard and commit some rash act. They soon rushed through the people, and by charging their bayonets in half-circles, kept them at a little distance. ..The mob still increased and were more outrageous, striking their clubs or bludgeons one against another, and calling out, 'come on you rascals, you bloody backs, you lobster scoundrels, fire if you dare, G-d damn you, fire and be damned, we know you dare not,' and much more such language was used. At this time I was between the soldiers and the mob, parleying with, and endeavouring all in my power to persuade them to retire peaceably, but to no purpose. They advanced to the points of the bayonets, struck some of them and even the muzzles of the pieces, and seemed to be endeavouring to close with the soldiers. On which some well-behaved persons asked me if the guns were charged. I replied yes. They then asked me if I intended to order the men to fire. I answered no, by no means, observing to them that I was advanced before the muzzles of the men's pieces, and must fall a sacrifice if they fired ...While I was thus speaking, one of the soldiers having received a severe blow with a stick, stepped a little on one side and instantly fired, on which turning to and asking him why he fired without orders, I was struck with a club on my arm, which for some time deprived me of the use of it, which blow had it been placed on my head, most probably would have destroyed me.

—Captain Thomas Preston

Analyze the passage and determine what sort of source it is.

A. context
B. point of view
C. secondary
D. primary

Why might this passage be considered biased?

A. It uses strong language.
B. The author works for the newspaper.
C. It is not biased.
D. It is from the point of view of the attacked.

Assessing Michigan Standard for Grade 8: Analyze point of view, context, and bias to interpret primary- and secondary-source documents.

• How would the fact that a computer company has found a less expensive way to produce their product affect the price?

A. They would be able to produce more.
B. It would lower the price.
C. The product would be of a higher quality.
D. It would raise the price.

Assessing Delaware Standard for Grades 6 to 8: Analyze how changes in technology, costs, and demand interact in competitive markets to determine or change the price of goods and services.

Social Studies Synthesis-Level Sample Questions

- Many people complain that the public park is in bad shape. What are two things you can do to improve the park, and what would these accomplish?

  Answer Rubric:

  > 1 point for thinking of two things to improve the park.
  > 1 point for explaining how they will improve the park.
  > Examples: organize trash to be picked up, plant trees, form a neigborhood watch to stop any crime, raise money to buy new playground equipment, form leagues to play sports in the park.

  Assessing West Virginia Standard for Grade 1: Propose solutions and investigate opportunities for public volunteerism concerning a local problem.

- Construct a line graph to display the amount of energy used over a straight five-year period from Kentucky.

  Amount of kW/hour

  <u>1978</u>
  Ohio 48
  Tennessee 54
  Virginia 25

  <u>1979</u>
  Mississippi 124
  Kentucky 64
  Ohio 99

  <u>1980</u>
  Tennessee 45
  Mississippi 17
  Kentucky 56
  Virginia 71

  <u>1981</u>
  Kentucky 43
  Ohio 88
  Maryland 94

  <u>1982</u>
  Maryland 37
  Kentucky 96
  Texas 119

  <u>1983</u>
  Tennessee 57
  Ohio 38
  Kentucky 56
  Kansas 64

  <u>1984</u>
  South Carolina 12
  Rhode Island 56
  Kansas 52
  Ohio 46

  <u>1985</u>
  Kentucky 29
  Texas 63
  Ohio 60

  <u>1986</u>
  Mississippi 39
  Kentucky 37
  Ohio 83
  Kansas 62

Answer Rubric:

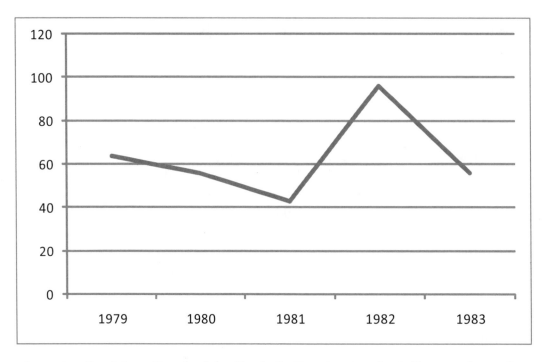

Assessing Louisiana Standard for Grade 3: Construct a chart, line graph, or diagram to display geographical information.

Social Studies Evaluation Level Sample Questions

- Your school would like to implement a school uniform policy where all students would wear the same clothes. Explain an advantage to having this policy. Explain an advantage to not having it. Which position would you take and why? How could you as a student best help to get the result you desire from the policy?

   Answer Rubric:
      1 point for providing an advantage. (Examples: Everyone will look nice; there won't be differences; no one will be made fun of because of what they wear.)
      1 point for providing an advantage for not having it. (Examples: It could be expensive for some families; it takes away student individuality; it would take time away from teachers to enforce.)
      1 point for taking a position and explaining why. (Example: I take the side of having school uniforms because I have friends who are made fun of because they don't wear the popular clothing.)
      1 point for saying students could help or hinder the passing of the policy. (Example: how students could organize a student petition against the policy; they could show support by going to a school board meeting.)

   Assessing Vermont Standard for Grade 4: Debate and define the rights, principles, and responsibilities of citizenship in a school, community, and country.

- What would have been the most important advantage to figuring out how to control the river in the Nile Valley? What might have happened if this technology had not been invented?

   Answer Rubric:
      1 point for explaining that it would have allowed them to grow more crops, enabling more people to eat and survive. Also, people could stay in one place and pass along ideas to the next generation.
      1 point for stating that if they had not learned to control the river, ancient civilizations might have started somewhere else and ancient Egypt would not have influenced us as much as it did with regard to math, medicine, government and religion.

   Assessing Utah Standard for Grade 5: Assess the influence of advancing technologies on the development of societies.

Science Knowledge-Level Sample Questions

- Which of the following is a change that happens slowly over time?

    A. volcano
    B. wind
    C. earthquake
    D. erosion

    Assessing Iowa Standard for Grade 3: Identify changes in and around Earth.

- Which of the following is a job a scientist would *not* do?

    A. teach
    B. record data at a wildlife preserve
    C. develop new baby food
    D. design clothing

    Assessing Indiana Standard for Grade 6: Identify places where scientists work, including offices, classrooms, laboratories, farms, factories, and natural field settings ranging from space to the ocean floor.

Science Comprehension-Level Sample Questions

- Why shouldn't someone look directly at the sun?

    A. It could make you dizzy.
    B. It could cause an accident.
    C. It is considered bad luck.
    D. It could cause injury to your eyes.

    Assessing New Hampshire Standard for Grade 1: Explain that people should not look directly at the sun because it is dangerous and may cause injury to the eyes.

- **Cell theory** refers to the idea that cells are the basic unit of structure in every living thing. Development of this theory during the mid-1600s was made possible by advances in microscopy. This theory is one of the foundations of biology. The theory says that new cells are formed from other existing cells and that the cell is a fundamental unit of structure, function, and organization in all living organisms.

    Which of the following is *not* part of the cell theory?

    A. Cells come from other cells.
    B. All organisms are composed of one or more cells.
    C. Cells are the basic units of life.
    D. Mutant cells can cause cancer.

    Assessing Kansas Standard for Grades 5 to 7: Understand the cell theory, that all organisms are composed of one or more cells, cells are the basic units of life, and that cells come from other cells.

Science Application-Level Sample Questions

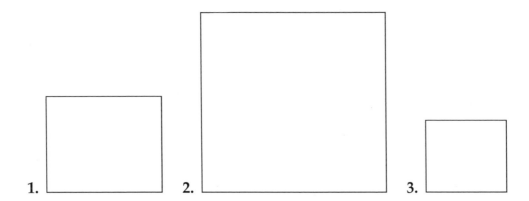

Place the following objects in order from largest to smallest.

A. 3, 1, 2
B. 1, 3, 2
C. 2, 1, 3

Assessing Missouri Standard for Kindergarten: Sort objects based on observable physical properties (e.g., size, material, color, shape, mass).

• Name two things that use electricity in your house. What would happen to your life if you didn't have the electricity to run these things?

Answer Rubric:
1 point for naming two items that would be found in a common house that run on electricity (appliances, heater, television, radio, clocks, etc.).
1 point for explaining how life would be different. (Examples: without television they would probably read more; without a refrigerator their food might spoil; without a stove they would have to cook food over an open flame.)

Assessing Florida Standard for Grade 2: Discuss that people use electricity or other forms of energy to cook their food, cool or warm their homes, and power their cars.

Science Analysis-Level Sample Questions

- A construction company has torn down a section of trees to build a housing development. What is a benefit to the ecosystem and what is harmful to the ecosystem? Make sure to explain your answer.

  Answer Rubric:
  1 point for answers that provide a benefit to the ecosystem. (Examples: might clear out damaged trees, provides shelter for human, garbage from new inhabitants can be eaten by animals.)
  1 point for answers that provide a harmful effect of the change. (Examples: destroyed homes of animals, pollution brought by homes of humans, destruction of plant life that provided food for organisms.)

  Assessing New Mexico Standard for Grade 9: Critically analyze how humans modify and change ecosystems (e.g., harvesting, pollution, population growth, technology).

- Which of the following is a chemical change?

  A. melting ice
  B. making Kool-Aid
  C. popping popcorn
  D. rusting

  Assessing Minnesota Standard for Grade 7: Distinguish between chemical and physical changes in matter.

Science Synthesis-Level Sample Questions

- Take a look at the following design. Right now the device causes a safety issue with small children and pets. How could you alter the design to make it safer? Would this change cause the device to work the same or would it affect the outcome?

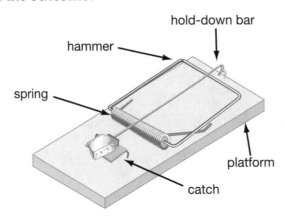

Answer Rubric:
1 point for altering the design of the mousetrap so that it is more safe. (Example: instead of a bar snapping down, a box could come down on top of the mouse, capturing instead of killing it.)
1 point for explaining how the change in design changes the way it works. (Example: now that the mouse isn't killed it could come back into the house.)

Assessing Maine Standard for Grade 4: Propose a solution to a design problem that recognizes constraints including cost, materials, time, space, or safety.

- If you were to make a plan to conduct an investigation, which of the following would you *not* want to include in it?

  A. testable questions
  B. systematic observations
  C. logical conclusions
  D. scientific relationships

Assessing New Mexico Standard for Grade 5: Plan and conduct investigations, including formulating testable questions, making systematic observations, developing logical conclusions, and communicating findings.

Science Evaluation-Level Sample Questions

- Determine which of the following slow processes would *not* have a long-term effect on the physical changing of the earth.

  A. weathering
  B. mountain building
  C. sea floor spreading
  D. global warming

  Assessing Rhode Island Standard for Grades 7 to 8: Evaluate slow processes (e.g., weathering, erosion, mountain building, sea floor spreading) to determine how the earth has changed and will continue to change over time.

- Read the following paragraphs then answer the questions.

  The status of the human embryo and human embryonic stem cell research is a controversial issue as, with the present state of technology, the creation of a human embryonic stem cell line requires the destruction of a human embryo. Stem cell debates have motivated and reinvigorated the pro-life movement, whose members are concerned with the rights and status of the embryo as an early-aged human life. They believe that embryonic stem cell research instrumentalizes and violates the sanctity of life and is tantamount to murder. The fundamental assertion of those who oppose embryonic stem cell research is the belief that human life is inviolable, combined with the fact that human life begins when a sperm cell fertilizes an egg cell to form a single cell.

  Some stem cell researchers use embryos that were created but not used in *in vitro* fertility treatments to derive new stem cell lines. Most of these embryos are to be destroyed or stored for long periods of time, long past their viable storage life. In the United States alone, there have been estimates of at least 400,000 such embryos. This has led some opponents of abortion, such as Senator Orrin Hatch, to support human embryonic stem cell research.

  Medical researchers widely submit that stem cell research has the potential to dramatically alter approaches to understanding and treating diseases, and to alleviate suffering. In the future, most medical researchers anticipate being able to use technologies derived from stem cell research to treat a variety of diseases and impairments. Spinal cord injuries and Parkinson's Disease are two examples that have been championed by high-profile media personalities (for instance, Christopher Reeves and Michael J. Fox). The anticipated medical benefits of stem cell research add urgency to the debates and has been appealed to by proponents of embryonic stem cell research.

In August, 2000, The U.S. National Institutes of Health's Guidelines stated:

"...research involving human pluripotent stem cells...promises new treatments and possible cures for many debilitating diseases and injuries, including Parkinson's disease, diabetes, heart disease, multiple sclerosis, burns and spinal cord injuries. The NIH believes the potential medical benefits of human pluripotent stem cell technology are compelling and worthy of pursuit in accordance with appropriate ethical standards."

How are ethics getting in the way of stem cell research? What are some benefits of stem cell research? What impact could this have on the world? Do you think the government should be involved in what scientists can and cannot do? Be sure to back up your opinion.

Answer Rubric:
   1 point for stating that the anti-abortion movement does not like the way the stem cells have been acquired because it involves the destruction of a human embryo.
   1 point for writing that the research could help develop cures for spinal cord injuries and Parkinson's Disease.
   1 point for writing that the research could help people with injuries to walk again, cure diabetes, and cause people to live longer with a better quality of life.
   1 point for backing up the opinion (Example: I think the government should be involved because it is providing a lot of the money for the research and should get a say in how it is used, or, I do not think the government should be involved because they are costing lives that could be saved by medical research they are regulating too much.

Assessing Oregon Standard for Grades 9 to 12: Evaluate ways that ethics, public opinion, and government policy influence the work of engineers and scientists, and how the results of their work impact human society and the environment.

15. Short-Cycle Assessment Checklist

The following checklist can be used when developing a short-cycle assessment:

Subject/Class_____

Grade Level_____ Assessment #_____

	Yes	No	NA
The assessment contains questions addressing all of the standards for the designated time frame on the Pacing Guide.			
The assessment contains the appropriate number of multiple choice questions as determined by the ratio on the state test.			
The assessment contains the appropriate number of constructed response questions as determined by the ratio on the state test.			
The assessment contains the appropriate number of response grid questions as determined by the ratio on the state test.			
The assessment contains the appropriate number of writing prompts as determined by the ratio on the state test.			
The assessment contains approximately 15 to 25 questions.			
The assessment contains higher-level thinking questions as determined by the Taxonomy Table and/or Leveled Pacing Guide.			
The reading level of the assessment is grade appropriate.			
Test vocabulary as determined by the state test is used throughout the assessment.			
The assessment is formatted like the state test.			
The assessment contains charts, graphic organizers, and reading passages specific to the questions.			
The standards being assessed are identified for each question on the assessment.			
Test administration has been standardized for the assessment.			
Scoring has been standardized (point values, specific answers have been given, etc...) for the assessment.			

16. Critical Thinking Flowchart

This flowchart has been designed to help you look at your assessment or insructional questions and determine whether or not the question is lower level or higher level. Use this to determine the level of your questions.

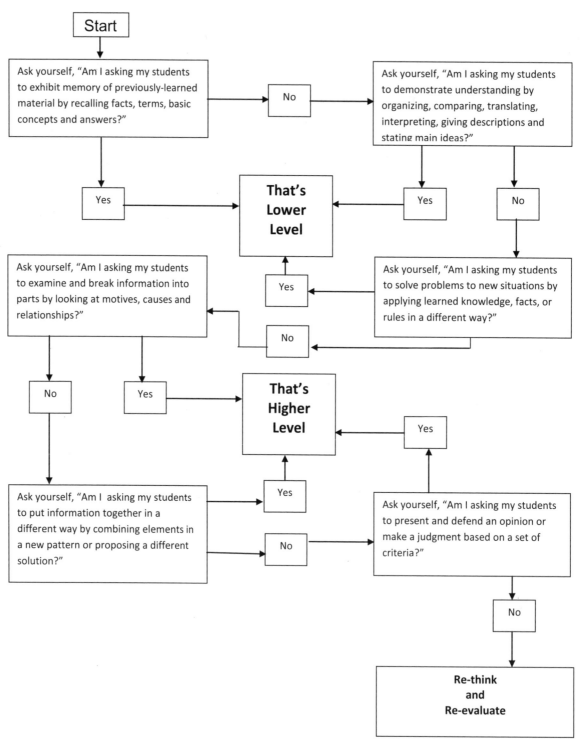

17. Developing Answer Rubrics for Critical Thinking Questions

When developing critical thinking questions for a formative assessment, it's important to have developed a rubric through which to filter the student responses. Most of the time these types of rubrics are question-specific.

The point value of the rubric will be dependent upon the point value of the question. If the question is a constructed response question that's worth two points, then the maximum number of points that students can earn will be two. Likewise, if the question is worth four points, then the maximum amount of points students can earn is four. An easy way to develop a rubric is to begin with the high end of the rubric and work backwards. To do this, you should have already studied your standard and determined that your question does indeed assess both the content and the level of your standard. Let's say for example, that your standard is:

"Analyze the difference between fact and opinion."

You know from studying the standard that the content being assessed is "fact and opinion." The level at which the standard is being assessed is *analyze*. This means that the question is going to go beyond simply identifying which statements are fact and which statements are opinion. Actually, the standard is asking the student to not only state the difference between fact and opinion, but also to look for relationships and generalizations that demonstrate the differences. Consider the following two-point constructed response question that assesses this standard:

Comparing a newspaper article (in which a reporter related a story) to a journal (in which a person who lived the story documented it), which would most likely be fact and which would most likely be opinion? Give an example to support your answer.

Of course one can tell from reading the question that it does, indeed, assess the content of the standard—fact and opinion. Now, look at the verb in the standard. The verb is *analyze*. Study the question. To answer the question correctly, are the students being asked to examine and find relationships between fact and opinion? Are they being asked to find generalizations and provide evidence to support the generalizations? The answer is yes. Now, go one step further to develop the answer rubric. What would be an exemplary answer, one that you would give the maximum number of points to and be assured that the students really did understand and know the academic content standard? We've written what we consider to be an exemplary answer below:

Comparing a newspaper article in which a reporter related a story to a journal in which a person who lived the story documented it, the newspaper article would most likely be fact and the journal would most likely be an opinion. I believe this because to be a fact, there must be provable action. To be an opinion, beliefs may be included that cannot be proved. For example, if a newspaper reporter were reporting the Holocaust, the article probably would include the names of the concentration camps, the locations of the concentration camps, and the number of people killed. These are all facts that cannot be refuted. The journal, however, written by a Holocaust survivor, may include descriptions of conditions, feelings of horror and beliefs about the politics of the Nazi regime. All of these are things that cannot be proved, but rather are the viewpoints of one person. That would make the journal an opinion piece.

After you have determined an exemplary answer, define the qualities that make it so. Do this by listing the qualities you see. For example, the answer above contains the following:

- correct capitalization
- correct punctuation
- complete sentences
- clear definitions of the terms "fact" and "opinion"
- specific examples of facts and opinions that relate specifically to the question
- supporting details that prove fact and opinion

These qualities now become the criteria for which the rubric can be created for the maximum point value answer. So, you would place the criteria in the column for the maximum point value. Then, you would need to decide upon the criteria for the other point values. The zero point answer criteria would be the opposite of the maximum point value answer. A sample answer rubric for the question above then becomes:

2 points	1 point	0 points
• Identifies that the news article would most likely be fact and the journal would most likely be opinion, while clearly defining "fact" and "opinion." • Gives examples of fact and opinion that relate specifically to the question. • Gives details in support of the answer. • Includes correct capitalization. • Includes correct punctuation.	• Does only one of the following: either identifies correctly that the news article would most likely be fact and the journal would most likely be opinion **or** gives an example of something that is written as a fact and something that is written as an opinion. • Gives an example of a fact and opinion that does not relate to the question. • Provides few details to support the answer. • Does not capitalize consistently. • Does not punctuate correctly. • Does not write in complete sentences with correct grammatical structure consistently.	• Does not answer either part of the question. • Is off topic. • Shows no understanding of capitalization skills. • Shows no understanding of punctuation skills. • Shows no understanding of writing in complete sentences with correct grammatical structure.

One last point about rubric creation—the best criteria for point value answers are "anchor" answers. Anchor answers are examples of each of the answers according to the point value that they would be awarded. Sample anchor answers make the criteria more clear as you are grading the assessment questions.

18. Detailed Answer Key

The following is an example of questions that assess critical thinking as found on a formative written assessment, along with the detailed Answer Key. Pay attention to the specificity of the Answer Key.

Question #1 : After reading the selection you could say that Hannah was as brave as a soldier. What does the metaphor "as brave as a soldier" tell you about Hannah? Justify your answer with examples from the text.

Question #3: Why was the 6th grade boy picking on the young girl? How did this make the young girl feel? Justify your answer. How would you feel if you were in her situation? Explain.

Question #6: Identify when Bode Miller first went skiing. If he had never gone skiing, how would Bode's life be different?

Question #10: Read the following paragraph:

> Mom, Dad, Hannah, and her brother, Gerry, loved to go out snowshoeing in the mountains after a heavy snow. The wide web of straps on the snowshoes keep them almost "floating" on top of the snow. Without the snowshoes, everyone would sink up to their chests in the deep snow when they are hiking.

After reading *Bodacious Bode Miller* and the above paragraph, what comparisons can you make between skiing and snowshoeing?

Ques.	Pts.	Answer
1.	2	1 point for stating Hannah was brave. 1 point for giving a textual example of Hannah being brave in the story (e.g., Hannah stood up to the bossy boy and told him he was wrong even though she was scared of him). The example must come from the text.
2.	1	D.
3.	4	1 point for stating that the young girl was far away from the bus driver (e.g., she was sitting in the back of the bus, etc.). 1 point for identifying a feeling (e.g., scared, frightened, angry; feeling must have to do with the situation of being bullied). Incorrect answer: any feeling having to do with being happy, cheerful, etc. 1 point for giving textual support for feeling; answer must come from the text (e.g., the girl began to cry). 1 point for telling how they would feel and giving an explanation (e.g., I would feel angry because it is not fair to bully others). The explanation must be included and must support the feeling.
4.	1	B.
5.	1	C.
6.	2	1 point for identifying that Bode went skiing for the first time when he was three. 1 point for providing an accurate explanation of how his life would be different (e.g., Bode would have never gone to the Olympics). Unacceptable Answer: " He would have been unhappy."
7.	1	A.
8.	1	B.
9.	1	C.
10.	2	1 point for each accurate comparison of the two snow sports (e.g., "They both take place in the snow," or " Both snowshoes and skis keep you on top of the snow").

19. Critical Thinking Data Chart

Fill in the chart below using only the data from the critical thinking questions on your formative assessment. You will need to identify these questions, along with their levels, ahead of time.

Question #										Total Pts.	Student %
Standard											
Level of Bloom's											
Student's Name											
Points Earned											
Possible Points											
Question Mastery %											

20. Class Profile Graph for Critical Thinking Questions

Complete the Class Profile Graph by recording the overall percentage for the critical thinking questions on your formative assessment.

Teacher _____   Subject _____   Grade _____   Assessment # _____

100%																						
95%																						
90%																						
85%																						
80%																						
75%																						
70%																						
65%																						
60%																						
55%																						
50%																						
45%																						
40%																						
35%																						
30%																						
25%																						
20%																						
15%																						
10%																						
5%																						

21. Proficiency on Critical Thinking Items Chart

List each student's name on the chart below, then tally whether or not they were successful on each of the critical thinking questions on the formative assessment. You will need to identify the critical thinking questions ahead of time.

Teacher_____ Subject_____ Grade_____ Assesment #_____

Student's Name	Analysis		Synthesis		Evaluation	
	Yes	No	Yes	No	Yes	No

22. Critical Thinking Item Analysis Graph

Identify each of the critical thinking questions on your formative assessment; list the question number, along with the standard and level on the graph below. Then, calculate the percent mastered by taking the number of points earned and dividing it by the number of points possible. Draw a line to the percent mastered to create a bar graph.

Teacher _____ Subject _____ Grade _____ Assesment # _____

Question #													
Standard													
100%													
90%													
80%													
70%													
60%													
50%													
40%													
30%													
20%													
10%													
0%													
Points Earned													
Points Possible													
% Mastered													

23. Questions to Ask When Analyzing Data with Regard to Critical Thinking Skills

- How much time did you spend teaching the different critical thinking skills?

- Was it enough time? Too little time?

- Was there any correlation between the time spent teaching critical thinking skills and the scores your students achieved on these items? What does this mean?

- How did you instruct the students with regard to these skills? Did you differentiate instruction? Did you use graphic organizers? How about writing prompts?

- Have you modeled how to answer higher level questions for your students?

- Were there any extenuating circumstances that could impact the data—calamity days, poor attendance, personal issues in the student's life, etc.?

- Were there any differences in the format of the questions with regard to performance (e.g., did the students score better on the multiple choice questions, or the constructed response questions)? What does this mean?

- Were there any individual students who did better than expected on the critical thinking items? Were there any individual students who did worse than expected on the critical thinking items? Why do you think this happened?

- How do these results correlate with what you see in the classroom? On the high-stakes test? On the national standardized test?

- What was the class mean for the critical thinking items? What does that indicate?

- Were there any specific standards on which the students performed better than the others? What does that mean?

- Were there any specific standards on which the students performed worse than the others? What does that mean?

- Was there one level of critical thinking on which your students were more successful than the others? Less successful?

- Could you have predicted performance on any of the items? If yes, what did you do ahead of time with that information?

- Were the critical thinking questions fair? Did they accurately assess the standard?

- Was there a common "wrong" answer the students wrote or chose? What does that mean?

- Were the results on your class Items Analysis Graph for the critical thinking questions significantly different from that of your colleagues? What does that mean?

- Are there trends across grade levels regarding the types of critical thinking questions on which the students are successful? Unsuccessful?

- Do you and your colleagues share ideas/strategies for teaching critical thinking skills?

- How much training have you had in the area of teaching critical thinking skills? Do you read books or attend professional development training on this topic?

- What are the instructional implications you can make from analyzing the data? What specifically can you do differently to change the results for the next time?

24. Instructional Time Distribution Graph

Think about how you distribute your instructional time, not according to subject matter, but according to the type of thinking you are asking your students to exhibit. Divide the pie chart below into percentages of instructional time with the whole circle representing 100%. The categories of thinking are:

- Review Activities
- Lower-Level Thinking Skills—Knowledge and Comprehension
- Application Skills
- Critical Thinking Skills—Analysis, Synthesis, and Evaluation

This is an estimate of your instructional time. When you finish, study the graph. If you are not satisfied with the amount of time you allocate to critical thinking skills, think about how you could redistribute your time.

25. Similarities and Differences Chart

Topic:_____

Similarities— How Things Are the Same	Differences— How Things Are Different

26. Analysis Chart

Steps of Analysis
#1. Describe what was learned.
#2. What do you have to know to really understand what was learned?
#3. In what order would you need to learn the concepts in step #2?
#4. Give another example of what you learned.

27. Synthesis Chart

Steps of Synthesis
#1. Describe what was learned.
#2. How did you learn it?
#3. What is a different way to do the same thing?
#4. What would happen if _____?

28. Evaluation Chart

Steps of Evaluation
#1. Describe what was learned.
#2. What is the question you are being asked to answer? What are the criteria for you to make your judgment?
#3. State your opinion and give reasons for it.
#4. Argue the opposite opinion.

References

Anderson, L., Krathwohl, D., (2001). *A taxonomy for learning, teaching, and assessing – a revision of bloom's taxonomy of educational objectives.* New York, NY: Longman.

Anderson, L.W. & Sosniak, L.A. (1994) *Bloom's taxonomy: a forty-year retrospective.* Chicago: National Society for the Study of Education.

"Are They Really Ready To Work? Employers' Perspectives on the Basic Knowledge and Applied Skills of New Entrants to the 21st Century U.S. Workforce." Prepared by a consortium of the Conference Board, Partnership for 21st Century Skills, Corporate Voices for Working Families, and the Society for Human Resource Management. April and May 2006.

Barton, L. (1997). *Quick flip questions for critical thinking.* Dana Point, CA: Edupress.

Blackburn, B. (2008). *Rigor is not a four letter word.* Larchmont, NY: Eye on Education.

Bloom, B. (1956). *Taxonomy of educational objectives: the classification of educational goals; handbook I, cognitive domain.* New York, NY: David McKay.

Bloom, B., Hastings, J.T., & Maudaus, G. (1971). *Handbook on formative and summative evaluation of student learning.* New York, NY: McGraw- Hill.

Lang, S., Stanley, T., & Moore, B. (2008). *Short-cycle assessment: Improving student achievement through formative assessment.* Larchmont, NY: Eye on Education.

Marzano, R.(2001). *Designing a new taxonomy of educational objectives.* Thousand Oaks, CA: Corwin Press.

Marzano, R., Pickering, D. & Pollock, J. (2001). *Classroom instruction that works.* Alexandria, VA: Association of Supervision and Curriculum Development.

McTighe, J. & O'Connor, K. (2005, November). Seven Practices for Effective Learning. *Educational Leadership, 63*(3), 10-17.

North Carolina Department of Education. US History end of the course exam.

Ohio Department of Education. Ohio Achievement Test (OAT).

Ohio Department of Education. Ohio Graduation Test (OGT).

Oregon Assessment of Knowledge and Skills (OAKS).

SAT (formerly Scholastic Aptitude Test and Scholastic Assessment Test). Mount Vernon, Illinois.

Stiggins, R., Arter, J., Chappuis, J. & Chappuis, S. (2006). *Classroom assessment for student learning.* Portland, OR: Educational Testing Service.

Stigler, J.W., & Hiebert, J. (1999). *The teaching gap: Best ideas from the world's teachers for improving education in the classroom.* New York: Free Press.

Texas Department of Education. Texas Assessment of Knowledge and Skills (TAKS).

Tomlinson, C. & Allan, S. (2001). *How to differentiate instruction in mixed-ability classrooms.* Alexandria, VA: Association of Supervision and Curriculum Development.

United States Department of Education. (2001). *No child left behind: Public law 107-110.*from http://www.ed.gov.

Wenglinsky, H. (2000). *How teaching matters: Bringing the classroom back into discussions of teacher quality.* Princeton, NJ: Educational Testing Service.

Wenglinsky, H. (2002). How schools matter: The link between teacher classroom practices and student academic performance. *Education Policy Analysis Archives, 10,* 12.

Wenglinsky, H. (2003). Using large-scale research to gauge the impact of instructional practices on student reading comprehension: An exploratory study. *Education Policy Analysis Archives, 11,* 19.

Wenglinsky, H. (2004). Facts or Critical Thinking Skills? What NAEP Results Say. *Educational Leadership,62 (1), 32-35.*

Wiggins,G., & McTighe, J. (1998). *Understanding by design.* Alexandria, VA: Association of Supervision and Curriculum Development.